WAITING
FOR
THE
ALL
CLEAR

WAITING FOR THE ALL CLEAR

BEN WICKS

GUILD PUBLISHING

LONDON · NEW YORK · SYDNEY · TORONTO

This edition published 1990 by
Guild Publishing
by arrangement with Bloomsbury Publishing Ltd

First published in Great Britain 1990
Bloomsbury Publishing Limited, 2 Soho Square, London W1V 5DE

CN 4159

PICTURE SOURCES

The Hulton-Deutsch Collection: pages 4 *bottom*, 5 *bottom*,
6 *top & bottom*, 7 *bottom*, 25 *bottom*

The Trustees of the Imperial War Museum, London: pages 1 *bottom*,
8 *bottom*, 12 *bottom*, 14 *bottom*, 15 *top*, 16 *top*, 25 *top*, 26 *top*

Popperfoto: pages 17 *top & bottom*, 18 *top & bottom*, 19 *top*,
20, 21 *top & bottom*, 22 *top & bottom*, 23 *top & bottom*,
24 *top & bottom*, 26 *top & bottom*, 27 *top & bottom*, 29, 30 *top*, 31

Topham Picture Library: pages 1 *top*, 2 *top & bottom*, 3 *top & bottom*,
4 *top*, 5 *top*, 7 *top*, 8 *top*, 9 *top & bottom*, 10 *top & bottom*,
11 *top & bottom*, 12 *top*, 13 *top & bottom*, 14 *top*, 15 *bottom*,
16 *bottom*, 19 *bottom*, 28 *top & bottom*, 30 *bottom*, 32 *top & bottom*

Typeset by Hewer Text Composition Services, Edinburgh
Printed and bound in Great Britain by
Mackays of Chatham PLC, Chatham, Kent

Acknowledgements

When it was suggested that I write this book my first reaction was surprise. To collect the stories needed from those who lived through the blitz on Britain in 1940–1941, I felt, would be an impossible task.

I was wrong. With the co-operation of many British newspaper editors, my appeal for readers with stories to tell resulted in more than a thousand letters. Without their help this book would have remained just another idea.

The German and English ex-pilots who so readily gave of their time and my editors, Charis Wahl in Canada and Penny Phillips and Caroline Taggart in England, who spent so many hours shuffling the words and pages, must also be thanked. Robin Fawcett, my remarkable researcher, deserves a special mention, as do my sisters, Doll and Nan, and, last but not least, my wife, Doreen, who once again showed endless patience and understanding.

For my mother, Nell

Contents

1	The War Overseas	1
2	After Dunkirk	10
3	The Battle of Britain	25
4	The First Raids	38
5	The Heroes Were Many	52
6	Making the Best of Things	85
7	Coventry	112
8	The Blitz Spreads	131
9	'The Most Unusual Christmas I Can Ever Remember'	161
10	Fire Over London	172
11	The Last of the Raids	182
	Postscript	207

1

The War Overseas

Britain declared war on Germany on Sunday 3rd September, 1939.

Aware of the threat posed by Hitler, Britain had started re-arming in the mid-1930s. Thousands of horrified cinema-goers had watched the German Junkers JU-87 make screaming dives on a defenceless population during the Spanish Civil War. But the Royal Air Force now had two new fighter aircraft, the Hurricane and the Spitfire, and was ready to take on the might of the Luftwaffe.

In 1938, Hitler had invaded first Austria, then Czechoslovakia. War began to seem inevitable. Appeals were made throughout Britain for volunteers to help with the problems that would arise at home. Lady Reading chaired the newly formed Women's Voluntary Service and urged women to follow her example; air-raid wardens undertook a house-to-house drive for recruits; 38,000 gas-masks were distributed throughout the country. There were so many posters asking for volunteers to join the Auxiliary Fire Service that regular firemen became uneasy about the possible threat of large numbers learning their trade. Telephonists, ambulance drivers, canteen staff would all be needed, and there would be plenty of work in the production of ships and munitions. More than a quarter of the nation's taxes were thrown into the defence budget, and at last the number of British aircraft coming off the assembly lines exceeded that of German ones.

By August 1939, recall notices had been issued in their thousands, and men were making their way to enlistment offices all over the country.

Alice Mulvey was camping in Devon with her sister, her husband Dick and a friend:

One evening it began raining and we decided to take a bed and breakfast instead of putting up the tents. While we were there that evening, we heard that all the reservists were being called up because of the grave situation that faced the country. 'That means me,' said Dick, whose reserve with the Grenadier Guards was up on 21st September. Next morning we went to Hereford to see my parents before heading back to London. That was the last time our whole family (six of us) was together.

Many of the schools began evacuation rehearsals months before the outbreak of war. These usually consisted of assembling the children in the playground and marching them off to the nearest railway station and back.

Gordon Tothill, now living in Canada, was attending a school that found a simple solution:

We did it without leaving the school. A teacher stood in one corner of the playground and pointed to the floor and said, 'This is the railway station over here.' We were then assembled in groups and made to march around the playground to the spot he'd pointed out, stop, turn around and go back to where we'd started and that was it.

Despite the Munich Pact and Prime Minister Neville Chamberlain's famous promise of 'peace for our time', Germany invaded Poland on 1st September. When Hitler then failed to respond to Britain's ultimatum, Chamberlain made a radio broadcast from Downing Street announcing a state of war. Shortly after this broadcast, the first air-raid siren sounded in London.

Oswald Garrison Villard, an American journalist living in London, made his way to the shelter nearest his hotel:

At the first one I came to it was 'women and children first', then the second, near my hotel, was full so I sat outside, convinced that it was a trial alarm.

It wasn't; a civilian aircraft had strayed into a restricted area. But within minutes the all clear sounded, the shelters emptied and women were back in the kitchen, concentrating on the Sunday dinner.

London began to take on the appearance of a city at war. Posters called for volunteers to fill sand-bags. Tin hats and gas-masks competed for

*attention and hundreds of civilians wearing various armbands patrolled
the streets ready to give orders at the first sign of danger. Every other
car appeared to sport a sticker to show that it belonged to a vital
service. Overhead, in the clear, bright sky, floated a flock of large,
silver-grey barrage balloons hitched to long thick cables, waiting for the
first German aircraft flying low enough to get tangled in their web.*

*All places of entertainment were closed and people were warned to
keep off the streets as much as possible. It was difficult to know how
serious the authorities were, as there was little that seemed threatening
outdoors.*

*With a black-out in force, the whole of Britain found itself living in a
dark world punctured by the cries of the local air-raid warden, 'Put that
bloody light out!' Black curtains covered every window. Entering a pub
after dark involved opening the door and pulling back floor-to-ceiling
drapes.*

*The government did its best to ease the strain of the black-out by
shortening the hours it was in effect. In November, 1939, the daily
black-out was cut by one hour, from half an hour after sunset until half an
hour before sunrise. Daylight saving time was extended by three weeks to
19th November, and began again a month early in February, 1940.*

*Although it protected civilians against threats from the sky, the
black-out increased the chances of meeting one's maker on the ground.
With no street lights, and shop lights and car lights down to a minimum,
the number of road accidents quickly doubled.*

*The threatened air-raids did not materialise. Cinemas and theatres
soon reopened, but football and other spectator sports, abandoned for
a while, now played to fifty per cent capacity. Most of the top players
had been called into the services and few spectators were willing to pay
to see inferior matches.*

*The music profession also suffered as bands found themselves with
seats left empty by musicians who had joined up. A young singer with
Ambrose's well-known band soon saw her saxophone-playing fiancé in
the uniform of the Royal Air Force. She found a song at a publishing
house and, as she explained later, 'It had a basic human message of
the sort that people want to say to each other, but find embarrassing
to put into words.'*

I was always careful of the songs I chose. I liked songs that had a
nice melody and songs that had a sensible lyric . . . nice words . . .
I used to spend days going around the music publishers listening
to songs, and they'd bring out stacks . . . and you'd sit there all

morning or afternoon going through the songs until you found
something that you liked.

If Vera Lynn liked it, the public loved it. We'll Meet Again *had just
the message that everyone wanted to deliver to a loved one: 'Don't be
too unhappy, we'll soon be together.'*

And why not? Surely the whole thing would be over by Christmas?

*Ration books had been issued at the end of September, 1939. Bacon,
sugar and butter were in short supply and people were told to register
with their regular shop before 23rd November. The cost of food began
to rise, and petrol rationing quickly followed.*

*People found these hardships difficult to accept: why were they being
asked to make sacrifices when nothing was happening? The news from
France indicated that the army had little to do but stare at the enemy
across a fortified wall.*

*With the old and unemployed suffering because of the rising cost
of living, the public increasingly wondered why the government had
decided to go to war at all. Morale was so low that several thousand
troops were deployed in London to help the police should the need arise.
Top-secret messages were sent to the army: back-up troops should be
available in case of emergency.*

*That particular emergency didn't arise, but for some months many
British people continued to feel that the war was not really anything to
do with them – unless it had taken their husbands, sons or brothers from
them. But across the Channel, Hitler's army was sweeping relentlessly
through France.*

*It was 7.30 a.m. on 15th May, 1940. Winston Churchill, Britain's new
Prime Minister, was woken from a deep sleep at Admiralty House,
London. The French Prime Minister was on the phone. He tried to
collect his thoughts and concentrate on the voice at the other end
struggling to speak English.*

*'We are beaten,' Reynaud blurted into the phone. 'We have lost the
battle.'*

Surely it couldn't have happened so soon.

*'The front is broken near Sedan; they are pouring through in great
numbers with tanks and armoured cars.'*

*Churchill flew to Paris immediately to see for himself and found
'utter dejection on every face'.*

*The British soldiers under the command of General Gort retreated to
the coast, passing over ground that had been fought over again and again
throughout history. German troops were everywhere. British men who*

*thought themselves safe were suddenly facing German soldiers behind
their own lines.*

*A wire arrived at General Gort's headquarters from Anthony Eden,
confirming the decision to evacuate the British army. 'Want to make
it quite clear that sole task now is to evacuate to England maximum
of your force possible.'*

*Gort immediately argued with the French that they should allow
their First Army to follow the British Expeditionary Force and make
for Dunkirk. On 28th May he established a headquarters in a beachside
villa at the western end of Dunkirk. From here he would direct the
greatest rescue of all time.*

*By 4th June, with Hitler's army just ten miles away, 338,000 troops
scrambled aboard ships of all sizes and made their way back to the
safety of Britain's shores. It was a turning point in the war, aptly called
by Winston Churchill 'a miracle of deliverance'.*

*The exhausted troops from Dunkirk could be seen all around the
country, making their way back home in their tattered uniforms.*

*Alice Cleary recalls she was ten years old and living in the seaside
town of Ramsgate in Kent:*

We lived in a large rented house where Mum took in vacationers
from London and other places for bed and breakfast.

In early 1940, the many rooms in our house were filled with
soldiers training and waiting to be shipped out to an unnamed
destination. We had quite a lot of snow that winter and my friends
and I would watch the soldiers parading down by the harbour. We
would tease them sometimes, and when the parade was over some
of them would catch us and playfully rub snow into our faces.

One day in May, our soldier friends went off as usual in the
morning and didn't return to our house again. Soon after, my
parents and I went down and waited behind the barricade near
the harbour to see the men come back from Dunkirk, hoping
to see a familiar face in the buses as they went by. Some were
wrapped in blankets and bandages, and most were holding cups
of hot drinks as they went to the hospital or home.

*Some evacuees, like the future Elsie Kingsland, found themselves on
trains leaving London as the soldiers were arriving:*

We stopped at a station and on the other side of the platform was another train and to this day I can remember the soldiers, some bandaged, waving to us — they were on their way home from Dunkirk. Us kids were loaded with goodies which our parents had given us, chocolate and biscuits etc, and we threw them on to the platform and the soldiers gratefully picked them up.

George Betts' brother was accustomed to going down to the base of the cliffs at Dover at low tide looking for drill bits from a local mining company. Just after Dunkirk he had a terrible shock:

My brother came running back home to tell us that there was a body on the rocks. The police were at once informed and with myself went to investigate.

To our surprise the dead man was over six foot and totally naked apart from his tunic that was wrapped around his head, being held there by the neck button. But the rest of this unfortunate man's body had been badly mutilated by crabs or some other means.

After unwrapping the jacket, that turned out to be Royal Marines, we found that the head and the features were perfectly preserved, although it was possible to see right through them as the jacket had turned the head almost luminous.

It was finally deduced that the body was one of the Dunkirk unfortunates. I never found out if he had been formally found to have a number or any identification to give to his grieving relatives.

Nan Wilson was just six years old when war was declared. Her father had gone to France and her mother was one of the thousands anxiously waiting for news of their loved ones as the retreat from Dunkirk was taking place:

Daddy came home. He had been one of the lucky ones picked up by a small boat. He had arrived home still in his very soiled, muddy uniform. We were all so happy to see him. He had only been home a few hours when there was a knock at the door.

His best pal had come to give Mum the news that Dad had not been able to make it, he had last seen Dad on the beach. Well, I

shall never forget the way those grown men fell into each other's
arms. It is very hard to describe. Dad's pal brought with him a
doll dressed in the traditional French costume. I remember it well.
It was from Nantes. My name is Nan and Dad had given it to his
pal to bring home to me.

*With the fall of France, Dover became the closest point to enemy
territory. The rescue of the BEF at Dunkirk had resulted in dozens of
ships making their way to the port and with new Luftwaffe offensives
filling the air above the town, it had become one of the busiest in the
British Isles. England's newest front line was soon known as 'Hell Fire
Corner'.*

*As a worker in the Eastern Docks of Dover harbour, George Betts
remembers the arrival of the boats from Dunkirk and the Battle of
Britain that followed:*

Small and large boats emptied their cargoes of British, French,
Belgium and other allied troops, it was easily seen just what they
had been through.

Once, when a motor torpedo boat started up its engines to roar
across the harbour to get out of the eastern entrance (the western
entrance was blockaded), a great number of these unfortunate men,
at once thinking the engine noise was German planes bombing
them, threw themselves to the ground in panic.

This in no way is a reflection on these troops, but was a good
indication of what they had been through during the Nazi blitz
whilst waiting on the beaches for the boats to return them to
England . . .

I saw one destroyer towed into the Eastern Docks with its stern
blown completely off and another one docked with its bridge
almost blown away; shell fragments mingled with blood plainly
showed that this gallant ship had been in a battle. Everyone realised
that it was now our turn to be invaded and being in the special
police, we were now on a war footing.

It was a bitter blow to us when we knew that the Nazi horde
were now only 25 miles from Dover . . .

Balloons were put up around Dover and its docks to ward off
the dreaded dive-bombers that had caused havoc with our troops

and the civilians, but it soon became painfully clear that we hadn't much in those days to stop anything.

Several anti-aircraft guns were manned on the promenade but these were very few as most of them had been taken to help London.

One morning, just after Dunkirk, I was examining the conveyor taking excavated chalk to the rocks adjacent to the eastern arm and decided to climb up into a cave where I knew a machine gun had been installed. Reaching it, I was confronted by several worried gunners who said they hadn't much ammunition and that the gun was only firing on a fixed line to just on the bend of the eastern arm pier. This was an example of the shortage of munitions.

As soon as the Nazis had established airfields in France they began. First the yellow-nosed Messerschmitts would zoom over knocking down all the balloons as well as machine-gunning the town and harbours and anyone seen moving.

Then would come the dreaded Stukas, mainly hitting the harbour, but now and again demolishing houses near the town . . . The air-raid shelters around Dover were particularly good with some being built into the cliffs directly under Dover Castle.

Despite the glorious summer, London was deep in shadow, dull and drab from the sacrifices being made to turn around a battle that was not going well. Even the decorative park railings were ripped away to do their bit for the war effort.

The lightning thrust of Hitler's armies across France had forced the British to desert their closest ally and make their way back to the limited safety of their home base. To Churchill's credit, he did not attempt to describe the defeat at Dunkirk as anything other than a major setback. Few doubted that in the coming months – perhaps years – they would find themselves in the front line of the battle to defend Britain.

After Dunkirk, the threat of bombing became greater. Churchill's Central War Room was built under the Foreign Office, lined with concrete for extra bomb-proofing. The Dorchester Hotel, with its bomb-proof shelter behind shatter-proof windows, was one of the safest places in London, and regulars like Lord and Lady Halifax, Duff Cooper and Somerset Maugham could still eat the finest of food there when work commitments prevented them escaping to the comparative safety of their country manors.

Many Londoners did not have the luxury of choice of residence, and began to look to the skies for the first signs of enemy bombers. Most of their spare time was spent gas-proofing rooms with cellulose sheets and tape or, if they were fortunate enough to have a garden, building an Anderson shelter.

Life in Britain had changed very little despite the news from France. In fact, a peculiar sense of strength pervaded the population with the appointment of Winston Churchill as Prime Minister. (He had become leader of a coalition government in May, 1940.) Ernest Bevin, a trade union leader and champion of the poor, along with other Labour members, made up the bulk of the new cabinet. For the British poor it appeared as if at long last their representatives understood their particular problems.

The news that France had finally signed an armistice with Germany cast gloom over Britain. To counter this, Churchill gave one of his greatest speeches, transforming a nation of disappointed souls to one of determination.

His lisping, booming voice ended with a statement that moved many to tears:

'Let us brace ourselves to our duties: and so bear ourselves that, if the British Empire and its Commonwealth last for a thousand years, men will say, "This was their finest hour".'

The King and Queen set an example by staying in London, giving people the confidence to fight on. King George VI spoke for many when he wrote to his mother after the fall of France that he now 'felt happier without allies that he was forced to be polite to'.

2

After Dunkirk

Hitler had many reasons to be satisfied with the way the war was going, yet he was uneasy. France had been brought to heel faster than even he had thought possible, but the British showed no signs of acknowledging how hopeless their situation had become. He had no real desire to invade Britain. Why were they continuing to hold out?

Reichsmarschall Goering was eager to prove the supremacy of his beloved Luftwaffe by sweeping the skies over Britain clean, before the army attempted to cross the Channel. The Royal Navy might still be the strongest in the world, but it would be no match for the power of Germany without an air force to support it.

By 1st August, Hitler had made a decision. Goering should have his way. Once the Luftwaffe had destroyed the Royal Air Force, the invasion, code-named Sea Lion, would take place.

Churchill was not impressed by the news. He knew that any attempt at an invasion 'would be suicidal'. Much more worrying was the possibility of a massive bombing attack, similar to those that had proved so successful in Poland. Waves of heavy bombers following tight 'V' formations of screaming Stuka dive-bombers were a devastating combination.

Unlike the German army and navy, the Luftwaffe was a new service full of daring young men anxious to establish themselves as the knights of the air. So far, they had only been used to support ground troops. In the coming battle they would be an army with wings, the first air force to set off into enemy territory without the help of an advancing army. No-one could predict how they would fare. Those attempting to stop their advance were just as uncertain.

Generals on the ground could study historical battles in the hopes that they wouldn't repeat mistakes made by, say, Napoleon. Air force leaders had no such assistance. As they pored over their maps, each devised a method of attack and defence for which there was no precedent.

The RAF was in the hands of Air Chief Marshal Sir Hugh Dowding. His objective was to hold out long enough for help to arrive in the form of enough aircraft and pilots to wear down the German air machine. British aircraft factories were desperately building aircraft to replace those being lost, and RAF flying training schools were working round the clock to produce badly needed fighter pilots. The Luftwaffe's target would not be shivering civilians and beaten troops cowering in trenches or the ruins of flattened cities. The British force would be leaping into the air to meet the enemy – an enemy far from home, over hostile territory and contending with unreliable weather conditions.

Goering's all-conquering force was ready. The plan was simple. First they would attack the fighter airfields in the south of England. Once these were rendered unusable, they would turn their attention to RAF bases further north.

They would need four weeks.

As the threat of invasion grew, young and old alike flung themselves into the task of defending their country. Anything that would help make life difficult for an intruder was put into place. (Unfortunately, it made it just as difficult for everyone else.) To leave a car unlocked or a bicycle unattended became an offence. Sign-posts, railway-station signs, shop names that gave the slightest hint of their location were removed. Bus destinations became the name of a local pub rather than a town or village. Many felt that the scheme was so successful that only someone with a good map, like a spy, had any hope of knowing where he was.

The ringing of church bells was forbidden, as this would provide the ideal warning system when the invasion took place.

Government departments struggled to keep up with the mounds of information and advice being released. The Daily Express *suggested that in the event of an invasion, people should leave the area. On the same day, the* Evening Standard *advised people to stay where they were.*

The image of a Britain filled with spies sprang up. Posters warned of the danger of loose talk. 'Be like Dad, keep Mum' screamed from walls everywhere. The press churned out stories of Germans and Italians who, although they had made their homes in Britain for many years, were by their very accents rendered suspect. Some newspapers advocated 'interning the lot'!

Caught up in this surge of hysteria, Churchill ordered a round-up of foreigners living in London. Police arrested 15,000 people classed as 'Grace C'. Most were Jews who had escaped the horrors of the concentration camps and were only too anxious to fight the hated 'Hun'. Some were scientists who could have made an important contribution to the war effort. Instead, along with thousands of others, they were hustled to converted holiday camps in seaside towns.

Renée Ascher found the reception far less friendly than she had expected:

I came to England with my mother as Jewish refugees from Vienna, Austria, just two months prior to the outbreak of the war. I came from an upper middle class, loving and protected family background.

As a consequence of the happenings of that time, and being hunted like an animal by the Nazis, my dad's only way out was to commit suicide the day after my twelfth birthday on 18th June, 1938.

I was placed in an orphanage and my mother worked as a volunteer nurse at the Jewish hospital, relentlessly writing abroad for help that we may escape to England. The freedom from oppression and fear . . . was akin to entering paradise.

My sponsors placed me in a boarding school. My mother, who had never had a paying job in her life before, was to be the matron, and since we couldn't speak English, she communicated with the headmistress in French. However, being an 'alien', she was soon forced to leave this coastal area and go to London to find employment elsewhere, so we couldn't stay together.

Eventually, Renée joined her mother in London:

My mother was asked to send me to Canada. While wrestling with the problem of coming to a decision, she dreamed of seeing children's heads bobbing in the sea. Their mouths were open and she threw bread to them. Upon telling this vivid dream to a friend, the friend said, 'Don't send her.'

In fact, the boat I would have sailed on was torpedoed and all the children perished.

Many classed as 'undesirable' were deported to the colonies. Known supporters of the Nazi movement were classified as 'Grade A' risks and imprisoned. Among these was Sir Oswald Mosley, the noted British Nazi leader.

The efforts to defend Britain also included the formation of a civilian army manned by those who were unacceptable for full-time military service. Anthony Eden, the newly appointed War Minister, made a plea for volunteers on BBC radio, suggesting that such a force could play a major role in holding off an invading army. The name for this new force, the Local Defence Volunteers, was changed by Winston Churchill; with his orator's genius for words, he christened it the Home Guard.

The Home Guard quickly swelled to a total of 250,000 men, unpaid and carrying out their duties after working hours.

During this time Pat Millett was based in London and had answered the call to join the Local Defence Volunteers:

At the time we irreverently called them Look, Duck and Vanish. After signing up we were mustered and formed into columns of three. A uniformed officer supported by a regular regimental sergeant major counted us off into companies, then platoons and finally into sections consisting of six men. I was the sixth and immediately made a corporal, a rank I still held when we finally disbanded. With this honour went a rifle and six rounds of ammunition — one for each of us, I presumed, in the case of dire emergency. An army great-coat and a tin hat, with instructions to report to platoon HQ where under a lieutenant we were to operate signals as soon as the warning was sounded.

Within a short while of being 'fell out', the warning sounded. Off I went as instructed only to find on arrival at platoon HQ no officer or platoon sergeant, so as senior NCO I felt it was my duty to take over first guard.

Putting on my great-coat and donning my tin hat I dutifully stationed myself in the at-ease position at the entrance to the HQ. Within minutes enemy aircraft in large numbers were observed approaching.

The sounds of guns were heard and then I got the fright of my life. From the enemy aircraft there appeared to be many, many white envelopes unfolding.

'Christ!' I thought. 'Bloody parachutists . . . hundreds of the buggers.' I was just getting ready to sound the alarm when an old sweat in my section who had been in the First World War appeared beside me and, looking up into the sky, commented on the ack-ack bursts.

Never having heard a gun fired in anger or seen a shell burst, I had mistaken them for parachutes unfolding.

Since the main purpose of the Home Guard was to repel an attack that never came, it is easy to assume that this remarkable civilian army served no useful purpose. This would be a mistake. Those involved were given an important opportunity to feel that they were 'doing their bit', and there is no question that, if the invasion had taken place, they would have given a first-class account of themselves.

Over most areas, barrage balloons were now more numerous than pigeons as they floated back and forth waiting for the first aircraft to engangle itself in their cable webs. Millions of sand-bags had been placed against various structures to protect them and ARP pill-boxes were sprouting like mushrooms throughout the country. These were manned by volunteers who had practised for months so that they knew what to do at the first sign of the enemy aircraft.

Emily Dimmock decided against attending evening classes at South-ampton University and began spending three nights a week at the Civic Centre on duty as a 'spotter' in the underground ARP headquarters:

This meant that in the case of an incident I would plot on the map where the bombs had fallen and what services were there by little coloured flags.

I had been practising this for several months before war broke out and had also attended first-aid classes, been taught to dis-tinguish between the various gases, taken gas-masks around to a good many houses, learnt that windows had to be taped with sticky paper strips in the hope that the occupant would not be showered with broken glass in the event of a bomb falling, how to deal with incendiary bombs with some sand and a long-handled shovel, and how to make a room gas-proof.

In the morning, the ladies of the WVS cooked us breakfast and we all went off to our various jobs.

In London, many taxis were now an ugly grey, having been splashed with paint before being recruited into the Auxiliary Fire Service. Advice was pouring from the radio and sheets of paper fluttered through every letter-box, telling how to protect oneself against the coming air-raids.

The black-out was enforced more strictly than ever. Audrey Sara remembers finding herself on Mutley Plain near Plymouth after dark and was having problems finding her way:

There was no moon or stars. I might as well have been down a coal mine. I had to walk about one and a half miles to my home and after bumping into trees, lamp-posts and falling off kerbs, I asked a lady if she could tell me exactly where I was.

The answer was, 'Hold my arm, dear. I'm blind and I do this walk every day.'

She knew every lamp-post, tree and kerb and she got me to my home in no time at all.

It was now impossible to cross a beach without becoming entangled in barbed wire. The British were ready for the invasion, and their resolve to continue the fight was growing stronger. Led by a cigar-chewing man with a mastery of the English language, they were going to see this war through to the bitter end – and win it.

A warm summer haze hung over the Channel, obscuring the view for both sides. Luftwaffe pilots at their new airfields in France, Belgium, Holland and Norway watched gasoline and ammunition arriving from Germany.

Some took an occasional flight to view the small green island across the narrow stretch of water that separated them, and found themselves wondering how the inhabitants could possibly feel able to resist the might of the German air force. Few of them realised that the two sides were not really mismatched. Germany was not in a position to blacken the skies with bombers, and in the pre-war years Britain had built its air force into a fighting machine unlike any the Luftwaffe had faced.

Hugh Dowding had served as a pilot in the First World War, and by 1934 had become a member of the Air Council for Research. Studying the armaments of the two new fighter planes, the Hurricane and the Spitfire, he realised that both could be improved by increasing their weaponry from four to eight guns. That decision had a dramatic effect when the battle finally took place.

Impatient and abrasive, he insisted on quality: once he demanded a change in materials for the cockpits, making the point that if Chicago gangsters could have bullet-proof glass for their cars, surely he should be permitted to have it to protect his fighter pilots.

His opponent was a large, ribald figure with a taste for colourful uniforms. But Hermann Goering's clown-like appearance concealed a sharp and active mind, and his jovial personality disguised remarkable self-control. Wounded in the stomach during the 1923 putsch, he had accepted morphine to kill the pain. As a result of the treatment he became addicted, yet cured himself by his super-human will-power.

Like Dowding, Goering had seen action in the First World War. One of Germany's most famous air aces, he had succeeded Baron von Richthofen as leader of the legendary 'Flying Circus'.

Now he had a new aircraft to lead, with one set of wings, not two, and infinitely faster. The ME-109, with a top speed of around 355 mph, was as fast as the Spitfire and faster than the Hurricane. It could out-climb and out-dive them both and its armament was heavier. True, its range was short and it was less manoeuvrable, but with a Luftwaffe pilot at the controls, this should not present a problem.

The remainder of Goering's aircraft were slow and ill-equipped for the coming battle. The force had been designed for a bombing and strategic role with flaws that had been overlooked by the weak opposition it had encountered in previous combats.

Britain also had a 'secret weapon'. Watson Watt, Superintendent of the Radio Department of the National Physical Laboratory, had developed a method of detecting approaching aircraft by the use of radio signals. The value of this 'radar' is impossible to measure. With it, Britain had found a vital new means of defence. Moreover, a related device made it possible for fighter pilots to report their positions to a control station on the ground in a clear voice.

It was probably the first battle to be named before it began. On 18th June, 1940, Winston Churchill rallied the people.

'I expect that the Battle of Britain is about to begin,' he warned. He was three weeks early, but the description was undeniably apt.

As the month of July slowly unfolded, Britain was as ready as she would ever be. She had a defensive line second to none. The area to be protected was ringed by the first radar chain in the world. Once any aircraft pierced its beam the message was passed back via various headquarters who relayed the information to the fighter pilots over a telephone and radio linkage.

Although the Luftwaffe had been experimenting along the same lines, they were far from perfecting the idea. Their strengths lay elsewhere, largely in the experience of many of their pilots. The Luftwaffe had seen action for three years before the war in Spain and followed up with action in Poland. Luftwaffe combat tactics were far more advanced than those of the RAF.

Rather than take advantage of this experience, however, the Luftwaffe delayed. Had they begun the battle before the end of June, they would have been facing a largely untried fighter defence with fewer than 500 Spitfires and Hurricanes, only half of which were stationed in the south east of England. When the last Hurricanes left France on 21st June, British Fighter Command was scraping the bottom of the barrel to find replacements for the 450 fighters and 430 pilots lost in the previous six weeks. Every squadron needed building back up to strength. By the end of June one third of them had still to be fitted with the device that would allow them to be distinguished from enemy aircraft on the radar screen.

But for Hitler it was a time of indecision. Should the Luftwaffe be acting in a military role, weakening the enemy before the invasion, or should the attack be a political move, hitting the civilian population with a repeat of the bombing attacks that had proved so successful in destroying the morale of Warsaw and Rotterdam?

The British strategy was easier to define. To destroy as many of the enemy fleet as possible but primarily to retain a fleet in reserve ready to tackle the enemy at the climax of the battle: the invasion.

To protect this reserve, Dowding secretly planned to withdraw many of his squadrons to the north of London if the southern bases should be too heavily damaged. One area of concern was the civilian population. How would they react to the heavy bombing from those aircraft who would inevitably get through?

Then there were the pilots themselves. For most of them it would be the first time they had seen action.

Many had enlisted overseas. Skeets Ogilvie would later become a squadron leader, but in August 1939 he had been a twenty-year-old Canadian anxious to get to England:

The RAF were taking anybody they could get their hands on. I think there were about sixty per cent of pilots from the Commonwealth . . . a lot of Canadians. I got called up on the Monday, had the medical on Wednesday and sailed on Friday.

The myth that aerial combat was a clean, chivalrous fight between two hanky-waving rivals had to be dispelled.

Many thought that aerial warfare was unchanged from the early days of the First World War, when unarmed pilots had waved when passing each other. The BBC commentator Charles Gardiner was no doubt thinking this as he stood on the cliffs of Dover and watched life-and-death aerial combat. Without a script he described the action much as he would a cricket match:

There's one coming down in flames . . . there somebody's hit a German . . . and he's coming down completely out of control . . . there's a long streak of smoke . . . ah, the man's baled out by parachute . . . the pilot's baled out by parachute . . . he's a Junkers 87 and he's going to slap into the sea and there he goes . . . sma-a-ash . . . Oh boy, I've never seen anything so good as this . . . the RAF fighters have really got these boys taped.

Strome Galloway was serving in an airfield defence unit at Odiham in Surrey:

The station building complex, one of Hore-Belisha's showpieces, had been officially opened only a year or so before by General Erhard Milch, a high-ranking Nazi airman, accompanied by Ernst Udet, a famous German World War 1 ace. To commemorate the event, a life-size oil painting of Milch in full Luftwaffe regalia hung over the officers' mess fireplace, actually the centrepiece of the mess decor. Now almost a year after Germany and Britain had gone to war against each other, Milch's haughty image in oils still glared down on the RAF and RAFVR officers as they took their ease in huge leather chairs, reading *Aeroplane* or leafing through *Tatler* and sipping their various drinks.

By now Milch was Hitler's Minister of Aircraft Production, working overtime to out-plane the RAF. Yet still his portrait graced an RAF mess.

Then one night bombs fell in the area. Odiham itself was badly hit and the airfield got its share. The tall Georgian windows of the officers' mess were shattered, the black-outs being sliced to bits, the lights going out and the airfield being pitted. Eventually order was restored. New black-outs were erected, the electricity came on and drinks were ordered from the bar.

Suddenly a young flying officer wearing the, at that time, relatively rare ribbon of the DFC, noticed that Milch's portrait had been knocked askew by the bombing. He got up from his chair, crossed the room and straightened the crookedly hanging picture.

From the twenty or so officers' mess members now relaxing after the upset of the raid, came a dignified applause.

The reality was that this was not a game and was no place for gentlemen. The winners would be those pilots able to catch the enemy from behind and shoot him in the back. Polish and Czech pilots had learned this lesson the hard way and they hated the Germans.

Skeets Ogilvie remembered one Polish pilot who flew with him:

He would tell us how his friends in Poland had been machine-gunned in the air after parachuting out of their planes. I remember saying to him one day, 'But you wouldn't shoot a German pilot coming down in a parachute, would you?' He said, 'Well, er . . . if no-one was looking . . .' Another time he shot a Junkers 88 down into the Channel and the crew were out on the wing. He went around and he was going to make sure that there was going to be no-one left on that wing.

He pressed the trigger and found he was out of ammunition, so he went around again and spent the next few minutes trying to knock them off and into the water with his wing-tip.

One Polish squadron was so anxious to get into action that it broke off a training exercise to shoot down a Dornier that happened to pass by.

Ronald Kellett, a London stockbroker who led the squadron, explained:

The trouble with commanding them was holding them back. They'd have rammed German planes if I'd let them. Time and again I had to tell them that one Pole for one German was not a good enough bargain.

Later, at the height of the battle, Kellett received a signal from headquarters:

The Group Commander appreciates the offensive spirit that carried two Polish pilots over the French coast in pursuit of the enemy today. This practice is not sound or economical now that there is such good shooting within sight of London.

Although efforts were made to inject a 'killer instinct' into the flyers, the 'sporting' analogy was obviously strong in the mind of the Group Commander.

Many on the ground felt the same way. Betty Martin came back from being evacuated:

When I arrived at the station at Gravesend there was an air-raid on at the time and I went straight to the nearest shelter without going home. During the Battle of Britain I had a whale of a time. As a teenager, my parents kept shouting to me, 'Come down into the shelter!' and we were up cheering our heads off at the fighting overhead. To me it was just . . . fun! We'd get on our bikes and go to where we thought the bombs had fallen and searched for bits of the bombs.

For the young Luftwaffe pilots scrambling in the heat of August the innocent look of green and peaceful England was deceptive. They realised that equally young pilots in their Hurricanes and Spitfires were gazing on the same scene, determined to defend it at all costs. The Germans in their single-seater aircraft faced a further problem. The aerial combat was being fought over enemy territory and their main concern was always to have sufficient fuel to get themselves home. And they knew nothing of the invisible weapon, radar. As the German pilots lifted their wheels and turned towards England, 'plotters' on the ground on the other side of the Channel had already locked them into a radio signal and were following their every move.

Margaret Woolrich was eighteen when she joined the air force and headed for Harrogate in Yorkshire, to be trained in secret.

My memories there were of the shoes, which were absolute torture. We did the marching bit at the Grand Hotel and then came down with a bump to the workhouse at Leighton Buzzard to complete the training. The ops room where we trained was under camouflage netting. It all seemed very secret and exciting.

We were trained on a large table with a map worked out in grids, and you were given a grid reference over the telephone. You had little magnetic arrows and a long rod with a magnetic head. You picked up these arrows with this rod and put them down on the correct grid reference. So you had this little trail of arrows, one lot for enemy aircraft and one lot for friendly aircraft. Looking back on it it was very simple, but at the time we were terrified of failing this test.

You got very nifty with these rods and eventually you could flick your wrist, throw them into the air and then catch them on the rod. You got prouder of doing this than you did of the actual plotting.

I was posted to Kenley Aerodrome. I didn't know then, but the plotters were a fairly privileged group. Because we did shifts and the work we did was very secret, we were excused most parades and we came in at odd times for meals, so we weren't terribly popular with the rest of the WAAF. Also a lot of quite aristocratic people found themselves plotting. The unpopularity of the trade was pointed out fairly forcibly my first night at Kenley.

I arrived in a raid in September 1940 to find a whole group of people under the table in the mess hall. Someone grabbed me and pulled me under the table where we all huddled. Eventually one of them said, 'What's your trade, luv?' and I said, 'I'm a plotter.' They said, 'A *plotter!* Well, if you are one of them toffee-nosed tarts, you can get out of here,' and they pushed me out to take my luck.

When I got there, the ops room had been bombed out recently and they were operating in a butcher's shop in Caterham. We would be bussed there. I don't know who it deceived because a whole group of uniformed people walking into a butcher's shop must have looked a bit suspicious.

This was just an emergency ops room and after just a few months we were moved into a much smarter one in an old rectory and that's where I spent the war.

It had been pointed out during our training that you only had to put an arrow in the wrong place and that could mean someone's life. So you did feel very bowed down by all this.

It was a very peculiar sort of existence for an eighteen-, nineteen-year-old, because the boys I went out with one night might be dead the next. We had one girl who always seemed to have fairly swift courtships with pilots who successively got shot down. Three fiancés ended up in the same POW camp, by which time there was a fourth on the books, I expect.

How the plotting worked was that there was one person manning headphones which were connected to radar stations on the south coast.

They gave you plots coming in over the sea. That's where you picked up most of the enemy raids. The observer corps posts around the country gave you plots from seeing or hearing enemy planes coming over. We wore earphones and when we heard the pilots we placed our arrows in the appropriate positions. It was terribly exciting. You felt you were at the hub of everything. The people you dealt with were in the newspapers every day. The pilots had the sort of status that pop stars have now. You would get the list of pilots going off on an operation so you would know that your friend was flying and then you wouldn't know until they'd all come back and been briefed that one of them was missing and then you would find out who it was.

Goering set about the destruction of Britain's Fighter Command with gusto, attacking airfields at Hawkinge, Lympne and Manston in the hopes of trapping planes on the ground, or at least making it extremely difficult for them to take off and land.

For those working in the area these raids could be unsettling. Many of the factories set up a spotting system of their own.

T. P. Dean was employed by a company in Maidstone, Kent, and spent most of his time watching the Battle of Britain from the top of a tower:

We had binoculars and kept watch, there were two of us, and pressed an alarm button to get the workers to the shelters as the planes got close. The reason for this was to keep production going as long as possible.

A heavy attack was taking place on Detling Aerodrome and I was in my bedroom at home and watching the planes as they bombed the drome. One plane left the scene and headed towards Maidstone. I leaned out of the window to get a better look at whatever this aircraft was and as he got closer saw it was a Junkers 87 and that he still had bombs slung and even as I saw the Iron Cross on the wings he pulled the release and the bombs started to fall.

In my panic I started to dash away from the window except for one thing. My braces were hooked on the window catch and I got about four feet away before I was pulled up short. By the time I had unhooked the braces the bombs had gone off about 250 yards away. The window shook but did not shatter. Lucky for me.

Being young and eager I dashed round to Marsham Street, Maidstone, where the bombs had landed. Two had exploded and a house was destroyed with two killed and a few injured. I soon found out that another two bombs had landed in Ashley Street and had not exploded. This is where Paddy came on the scene.

Paddy, whom I knew well, was a private in the Royal Engineer bomb-disposal team stationed in Union Street where they had facilities for dealing with bombs. Paddy was sent by his sergeant to check the two bombs that had landed and then took matters into his own hands.

One bomb in particular was only a fifty-kilo and had penetrated only to the fin, so Paddy decided to deal with it himself. He dug the bomb out in about half an hour and Paddy, who was a massive man, with hands like shovels, picked that bomb out and decided to carry it to the Union Street depot which was about 200 yards away.

He sweated up the road with the bomb. About fifty yards from the depot there is a pub called the Rifle Volunteer. A pub which is still there. The landlord at the time was a Mr Whitley, a veteran of the First World War. Paddy was getting tired and gently lowered the bomb to the pavement and went into the bar to ask the landlord for a pint. The landlord, who by now knew what was outside, said, 'Paddy, you can have all the beer you want, but take that bloody bomb to the depot first.' So Paddy duly obliged and delivered the bomb to the depot before coming back for his well-earned pint.

Poor old Paddy never got a court martial or a medal for this episode and sadly a few months later we had a letter from his wife in County Sligo asking if we knew where Paddy was. It seems he had gone to London on leave and disappeared and we never heard from him again.

Watching these battles over the Channel was stirring stuff and those who felt that the outcome of each combat could result in the loss of their freedom found it difficult not to get excited. Marie Lewis was twenty years old and living on the coast in 1940:

One evening I was standing beside our wired and sand-bagged shores and saw our planes doing battle over the sea on our behalf to keep the enemy at bay. The odds were so much against them. When they returned, if they had had a good victorious fight, they would roll over and over doing a victory roll.

I know they couldn't see or hear me, but I clapped my hands and with tears streaming down my face I would call out, 'God bless you. Well done, boys!'

The stories of German pilots flying low overhead were many. Violet Phillips remembers being on the golf course when a German bomber crashed nearby:

So many local people were killed rushing over to get souvenirs when it exploded and blew up. The German pilot was buried in the tiny churchyard of St Paulinus in Crayford, Kent. He was buried at the far end of the churchyard with a tiny wooden cross away from all the others.

Marjorie Ulph was living in an old railway goods wagon to get away from the air-raids and arrived home to find her mother jumping with excitement:

'Guess what,' she said. A German pilot complete with swastika had flown low over the adjoining field and the pilot had waved to all the people.

3

The Battle of Britain

By the end of the first week in August, airfields throughout France, the Low Countries and Norway were throbbing with some 3,500 planes anxious to take to the air and deliver the final blow against the stubborn British.

Against this number, the Royal Air Force had built a force of 720 operational Spitfires and Hurricanes. Yet however satisfactory the number of planes pouring off the assembly line might be, there was a much greater need: fully trained pilots.

It was estimated that it took fifty times as long to train a Spitfire pilot as it did to build the plane, and once built and operational a Spitfire with a dozen holes in it could be repaired and sent into the sky once more. A pilot with bullet-holes was not as easy to get back into the battle. Even those without visible wounds were scarred by nervous exhaustion and needed to rest before climbing back into the cockpit.

Many had difficulty sleeping. Meals were constantly interrupted and many half mugs of tea were left standing in the huts as the planes roared down the runway. Dowding did his best by rotating his pilots, but all too often the new boy who had arrived as a replacement found himself on his first flight tumbling from the sky in flames.

Bobby Oxspring was 21 and thought of himself as a veteran:

You had to be able to fly without thinking about it. It's — what shall I say — like playing the piano. You can't be a musician while you still have to look for the keys. And about that time, about the end of August, we were starting to get these boys as replacements who hadn't really finished their training. They still had to think about flying the aircraft. And it was pathetic, terrible, to see them go down, right away, in their first flight sometimes. You just didn't have to brood on that sort of thing, or let the others brood on it either.

Bruno Petrenko is now a retired Canadian businessman who was a 22-year-old ME-109 pilot in 1940. He had volunteered to fly in 1939 when there was an opportunity to become a fighter pilot and had less than a year's training when he reported to his unit in the Calais area. He made his first flight on 31st August:

I was not supposed to be in on the flight since I was a beginner and they didn't want to take me since the flight was to be over England. But another pilot who was supposed to be on the flight had suddenly some stomach pains and had to rush to the toilet.

Everybody was waiting for him to come out but he didn't come back so they said, 'Well, you had better take his place.' So I was on the mission by chance.

Shortly after crossing the Channel he found himself under attack and the protective shield just behind his back was hit:

It was the first time I had experienced this . . . it was a kind of ticky, ticky, tick . . . but it made me feel good that it had protected me. Anyway, what I did was evade whoever was firing at me by nose-diving. Now, I thought, I've got rid of it, so I climbed up again trying to catch up with the unit. I remember thinking, Well, this isn't so bad . . . The protection had held . . . but I was still climbing and suddenly there was a second attack from behind. It was so fast that I couldn't evade before it came . . . at least, I as a beginner couldn't. Suddenly he was there and immediately I went down again. While I was diving I thought, Well, what do I do now?

Some pilots said that in such a case you just go down to tree-top level and go home . . . but I thought, Well, that sounds too easy, so I decided to climb up again . . . which was a big mistake that an experienced man would not have made.

Then as I was climbing again suddenly I was attacked from below to the right-hand side. Someone who was more at home playing these games had come from below from the right-hand side. In this area there was no protective armour so it was a real problem.

The glass from the cockpit was splintering, the instrument panel splattered and now I was really hit . . . or many hits. Somehow at that point I blacked out.

When I came to I found myself in a vertical dive and what I noticed was lots of noise, a kind of fluid coming from the side of the plane and what struck me was that the ground was approaching very fast. I realised that I had to catch the plane immediately and get it out of the dive. I did and in doing so my blood rushed from my head and I blacked out again. When I came to I found I was at tree-top level with little power left in the machine. It could still fly but with no power. I was now very, very low and had to look for somewhere to land.

At this stage I looked around and found that there were two Spitfires behind me and they were shooting occasionally, but I guess it was difficult to shoot at me because I was going so slow and was not flying in a straight line. I don't know whether they didn't shoot me because they saw I was in a difficult situation . . . anyway, I just saw an English park-like landscape, some bushes and trees. There was a group of trees ahead of me and I said to myself, Well, gee, what I have to do is to try to get enough speed by flying directly at the trees and then hope that I have enough speed to jump over them and then go down. I did this and then blacked out once more.

Petrenko was found by British sergeant John Clancy who was with a searchlight unit:

I was stationed between Brentwood and Epping in Essex and was driving around when I heard that there had been a German aircraft shot down in the area.

I jumped into my van with a couple of men and took off. We soon located the aircraft about half a kilometre from the Brook farm house. It was on its back . . . nose well into the ground (actually the nose had broken away and was ninety yards away still burning).

The tail was cocked up in the air with the plane lying at a 45 degree angle. The airscrew had bounced two or three hundred yards away. The wings had broken off the plane from the sides.

On approaching it could be seen that the pilot was hanging upside down in the cockpit, bleeding and unconscious. The hood of the cockpit was shattered badly.

I set out in the first place with my rifle breathing fire and slaughter, but when I saw this poor gory head hanging there the rifle went down on to the ground and I started to wriggle my way under the plane to get the victim out. I have no clear memory of the actual extraction, but after a rather hairy time underneath the plane on the flat of my back, I finally got the pilot out and, with the aid of some water from the van, I tried to bring him round and clear up his face.

He seemed to have head injuries. The first words he spoke were, 'Spitfire?' I said, 'Yes!' The next thing he said was, 'Why are you being so good to me?' This stumped me and I came back with a rather fatuous reply, 'I don't know. You might have been one of our boys, mightn't you?' Then he looked up at me and said, 'How far to the sea?' To which I could only reply, 'Too far!'

Petrenko was then taken to St Margaret's Hospital in Epping:

I was there for ten days. There was always a British soldier with me, making sure I didn't escape. The nurses and everyone were very kind.

After the ten days I was ready to go and my head was dressed with an impressive bandage, like a turban. I put on my uniform and a young British officer and soldier took me by train to London. On that trip I found out that the names of all the stations that we passed through were 'Bovril'. I didn't know that they had removed the names and left the advertisement.

We then left the station in London and we got into a car and the idea was to go to a POW-collecting camp near Hyde Park . . . on the railway trip I had managed to talk to the British officer. My English wasn't very good, but we discussed history and things. Anyway, in the limousine, he suddenly said, 'By the way, have you ever seen Buckingham Palace?' and I said, 'No.'

He said, 'Well, would you like to see it?' and I said, 'That would be terrific.' Then he leaned forward to the driver and said, 'All right, now go by Buckingham Palace.' We then drove up to the gates and it was around the time of the changing of the guard, so we sat there and watched the changing of the guard . . . it was a wonderful, nice and warm gesture.

The straits between Dover and Calais had become such a hot-bed of German activity that the British decided to withdraw the destroyers that sat in the harbour. Convoys making their way through the narrow channel would do so only after dark.

The crews of the first of these convoys, some two dozen coal ships, were assembled in a dance hall in the seaside town of Southend and told that from now on their orders would be given by the Admiralty. It was a matter of prestige. The Germans claimed that they controlled the Channel, but this coal convoy was going to prove them wrong.

As the convoy manoeuvred itself out at dawn, a group of German torpedo boats came out of the half-light and sank three of the ships. Later in the day, the dive-bombers attacked out of a ceiling of low cloud. Fortunately some of the ships carried barrage balloons that held the dive-bombers at bay.

At midday, a large force of Luftwaffe fighters escorted dive-bombers over the target. Four merchant ships were sunk and a further three badly damaged. The remaining ships scattered and attempted to reassemble off the Isle of Wight, but found 82 JU-87s with a large escort of fighters ready to finish them off. Only four of the original twenty ships made it to Dorset.

A German pilot in the water would have had the benefit of flares, sea dye, yellow skull-cap and one-man dinghy, plus the chance of being spotted from the air by one of the many float planes that were part of the German search and rescue programme. The British had no such air-sea rescue organisation, and few survivors of the convoy were recovered.

Tubby Mayne was 39 and had the extraordinary distinction of having enlisted in the First World War: extraordinary among fighter pilots, many of whom were under twenty. He was flying a Spitfire when the German air force began to make its attacks on the Channel convoys. Twenty years later, Mayne told the Sunday Times *what it was like:*

Convoy escort duty wasn't so bad when you could find the convoy. But there were bad days, even in that fine summer, and looking for ships in low cloud and rain, and damned great waves, green ones, just below you – well, all you could think of was your Mae West. Do you know, we were supposed to wait until we were in the drink, and then unscrew the nozzle and blow the thing up with our own lungs, and then screw it up again.

It's fantastic to think of how primitive our equipment was. After all, the whole battle was fought with rifle-calibre bullets. But the Spitfire and the Merlin engine, they were superb. They were what gave us confidence. You got in that cockpit and shut the canopy and you felt you were in a fortress and no-one could get at you.

More and more ships were sunk as the Luftwaffe increased its attacks on the Channel convoys. George Betts and his brother had a front row seat at Dover:

We were standing beside some tunnels at the foot of the cliffs when, without warning, two Messerschmitts which had been converted to carry one bomb each swooped down over our heads and loosed the bombs at the huge naval supply ship *Sandhurst* that was moored quite close to us. She had a destroyer named the *Codrington* alongside her, being refuelled.

At once all hell broke loose and me and Colin, picking ourselves up after the blast had knocked us down, were nearly knocked down again as workmen and sailors ran into our tunnel. Afterwards, we found that the supply ship was on fire and the destroyer had been almost broken in two alongside her . . . the navy managed to tow the crippled *Codrington* away, but she was hit by bombs as she made her way into the Thames estuary and was sunk.

The next phase of Goering's campaign was day and night bombing of the British air industry, to ensure that the air force he was crushing could never be replaced. The operation was to begin on 10th August, code-named Alder Tag *(Eagle Day). But first the British early-warning radar systems had to be put out of action. Fleets of Stukas, Dornier and*

Heinkel bombers protected by ME-109 fighters roared across the white cliffs of Dover to attack the installations that dotted the south coast of England. The huge masts made an easy target and the opening raids damaged four stations and destroyed another. Once again, the British pilots threw themselves at the raiders.

Goering decided to cancel future attacks on the early-warning system. Rather he favoured a massive attack against the airfields and gave the order for 1,485 aircraft to take to the air on 13th August. It was a disastrous move. Bad weather meant that planes had to be recalled, but many were already on their way and did not receive the order. Fighters which did hear the recall made their way back to base, leaving bombers undefended.

By mid-afternoon the weather had improved and Goering's planes set off once more across the Channel. Their chosen targets were thought to include eleven fighter stations, but in fact only one was a fighter station and the raiding bombers missed it. Late in the afternoon a fighter unit successfully lured a group of Spitfires away from a planned bombing attack on Detling. Sixty-seven airmen lost their lives during the attack and 22 aircraft were destroyed on the ground.

The Nuffield Spitfire factory was attacked by a group of German bombers that flew in under cover of darkness and unleashed 211 high-explosive bombs.

By the end of the day, 46 German aircraft had been shot down, compared with thirteen Royal Air Force planes, but an additional 47 British fighter planes had been destroyed on the ground. It had been costly for both sides. Goering ordered a day's respite so that he could orchestrate his next attack.

As the weather cleared on the morning of 15th August, 1,800 sorties involving 500 bombers made their way towards a 500-mile stretch of the English coast. The radar was waiting for them, and Dowding was particularly pleased with the way the women performed at their cathode-ray tubes. Huddled in five closely guarded huts along the south coast, they worked tirelessly at their secret apparatus, marking enemy aircraft for destruction long before they reached Dover.

Calmly and deliberately they recorded the progression of V-shaped blips and after sifting and assessing each mark, distributed long streams of transmuted data to the eagerly waiting fighter pilots. Even as the German planes lifted into the air above France, phones were already ringing warnings to the British fighter stations and anti-aircraft posts back in England.

The little-used Lympne airfield in Kent caught the first shower of bombs: hangars burst into flames, workshops fell apart, and dirt and debris rose into the air from an almost deserted runway.

Overhead, planes were weaving their white vapour trails above the fields. Occasionally a puff of smoke would become a glow of flame and the nose of an aircraft would dip and then begin to spiral slowly towards the ground. The white canopy of an escaping pilot could also be seen swinging back and forth, relieved to be away from the airman's greatest dread — fire.

Observers on the roof of a Maidstone church in the heart of Kent cheered wildly as a German aircraft burst into flames and were about to ring the church bell in celebration when someone realised that this was the signal for an invasion.

The Spitfires and Hurricanes came as a shock to most of the Luftwaffe flyers, who were under the impression that the RAF was seriously short of planes and pilots. The women working over the large maps and boards in the operation rooms began to push the disks slowly towards the east as the battered German force made its way home.

Elderly observers on the coast lowered their binoculars and prepared to make their way back to nearby villages. There would be incredible stories to tell in the pub tonight. The puffs of the ack-ack that had followed the returning Luftwaffe were dispersing, drifting like balls of cotton wool along the Channel coast.

Next morning the corner newspaper-sellers were on the streets of London. In large chalk letters the news '1 8 5 JERRIES DOWNED' gave civilians just the lift they needed. Although the figures were vastly exaggerated (sixty was the official number), the RAF had, in that single day, in Churchill's words 'cut to rags and tatters separate waves of murderous assault upon the civil population of their native land'.

It was an important victory for Britain and had a deeply demoralising effect on the Luftwaffe bomber pilots.

That day the German aircraft based in Norway made their one and only major daylight attack without the protection of a fighter escort. They were slaughtered on the long flight home. One hundred other Luftwaffe planes made their way from the north to the Thames estuary; Number 11 group took off and tackled them over the southern ports of Folkestone and Deal. Two to three hundred more German aircraft crossed Hampshire and Dorset. In Scotland, a hundred Heinkels and seven ME-110s were spotted approaching the Firth of Forth. Just south of the border, Sunderland sirens warned of the coming raid and by the time the all clear was sounded 24 houses lay in ruins.

As the day wore on, the fierce battles raged high in the sky and all that could be seen were the wind-blown smoke-trails of dog-fights that had been.

First the Stukas, then their escorting fighters turned for the safety of the French coast. Behind them small bands of Spitfires and Hurricanes snapped at their heels.

The women at their radar tubes followed the fleeing planes, checking not only their course but the speed and height of the limping survivors. Suddenly they noticed the tell-tale blimps of a new formation of German fighters waiting to ambush the pursuing British as they approached the Pas de Calais. The British fighters were immediately ordered to break off the chase and return to base to rest and refuel.

In the days that followed, the battle for air supremacy crept closer to London. Croydon Airport, an obvious target, was attacked. A great deal of damage was done to the airfield itself and to the surrounding houses and factories.

Mollie Fairey recalls nursing at the Croydon General Hospital. Her mother was a district maternity nurse in Penge, south east London. Mollie remembers that one morning her mother was out visiting mothers and their babies:

Many mothers had their babies at home in those days. At 1 p.m. she got home for lunch. By 2 p.m. she was dead with the house bombed to pieces. I knew nothing of this as we were very busy in the hospital.

I went home for my Monday off-duty, 9 to 12 a.m., and found my house completely flattened.

I was nineteen years old and didn't know what I should do, but eventually went to the police station.

My mother wasn't found for three days and then the funeral service had to be rushed through as there was an unexploded bomb in the churchyard.

Jean Gough lived in Wallington, Surrey, close to Croydon Airport:

I worked in a chemist in Wallington High Street and one evening at about five o'clock some fighters came over doing the victory roll (which they often did). My boss and I and others were watching from the shop doorway when there were loud explosions (it was said afterwards that the German pilots had followed our fighter pilots back. It was also said that Croydon was an easy target for the pilots who had been civilian pilots in and out of Croydon).

My boss, who was an auxiliary fireman, grabbed his tin hat and made for the fire station, telling me to go opposite to the air-raid shelter in the corn chandler's cellar. When I arrived there the elderly owner asked me to wait whilst he got the straw out of the cellar (he sold rabbits) and he would sweep it out.

Meanwhile a bus that passed the top of our road pulled up and asked if I wanted a lift. (Imagine this now, no doubt the driver would put his foot down.)

When I arrived home my mother said that my dad (who was a stretcher-bearer in the ARP) had gone to the airport to see if he could help. (Over 300 people were killed at Bourjois perfume factory alone.)

That night I had a date with a Canadian sergeant and he should have met me at work at 5.30. He arrived at my home at ten o'clock and said he was on a trolley that passed the airport three minutes before the bombing (buses ran every three minutes then). The one after his had a direct hit and all the people had to alight because the power lines had been destroyed. He and all the other males present and some women went back to help get the casualties out.

When my father arrived back in the early hours, he said that relations and friends of the people trapped and killed were so frantic to get to the casualties they hindered the ARP, and firemen had to train their hoses on them so they could get on with their job.

Someone else living close to Croydon Airport was Ethel Sumbler. She was cycling past Purley roundabout on her way home when a large fleet of bombers approached the town:

Nobody took any notice as we were used to seeing large formations of planes, as Croydon was the home of London Airport at the time.

Everyone thought the approaching aircraft were ours. The planes turned over my head towards the airport and when I looked again they had released their bombs, falling just like rain. In blind panic

I jumped off my cycle and ran, everyone else doing the same. Windows were falling out and buildings were crumbling and dust thick all around us.

People were just leaving work and were caught out, not being able to get to any shelters. 63 people were killed, 45 seriously injured, many more being slightly injured. Many were buried in a mass grave as they were unidentified.

The raid was all over in fifteen minutes and not until some time after the last bomb was dropped did the alert sound. The reason given at a later date for the delay in sounding the siren was mistaken judgement on the part of officers operating the system.

Some of us did get to a shelter when it was all over and I fainted away with shock. But I was grateful to be alive.

16th August saw no let up in the pressure from the Luftwaffe. Another 1,700 German aircraft came at Britain, among them two JU-88 bombers that dived out of an overcast sky and scored direct hits on the aircraft hangars at Brize Norton. All 46 aircraft that were housed in the hangars were destroyed.

There were acts of great heroism on both sides during these remarkable days. Flight-Lieutenant J. B. Nicholson of 249 Fighter Squadron was awarded the first of the Fighter Command's VCs. As he weaved and bobbed in the middle of dozens of enemy aircraft his Hurricane was struck by four cannon shells. He was wounded and his petrol tank, which had been hit, began to pour flames into his cockpit. He was about to bale out when he saw an ME-110 and immediately got back into the burning plane to get the German into his sights and fire a cone of rounds into the fighter. Only then, burned and bloodied, did he parachute from his plane. As his feet touched the ground an overly excited Home Guardsman shot him in the rear end.

Skeets Ogilvie, now a Spitfire pilot, reported to his squadron and found a hell of a mess:

When I got to the station, Middle Wallop, the Germans had plastered the aerodrome a few days before and blown a hangar. A big door had come down on two little guys running for their lives and this god-damn steel door came down and they became part of the tarmac.

By 18th August the battle had begun to turn around. Almost a quarter of the German bomber strength was made up of the slow-moving Stuka dive-bombers which had met their match in the faster Spitfires and Hurricanes. Alarmed at the casualty rate among the Stukas, Goering first increased their fighter escort, then withdrew them completely from the battle.

However, the British pilots who survived were red-eyed and exhausted, and the bombed factories had not been able to replace the lost Hurricanes and Spitfires. Pilots were soon being transferred from the Fleet Air Arm and Bomber Command. The flying course was cut back drastically: a pilot now had only two weeks between learning to fly and going into combat. And that just wasn't enough.

Bobby Oxspring had been on week-end leave when his squadron had been posted to Kenley, south of London. He described the situation to the Sunday Times:

It was nearly a week before I caught up with them. By that time, six of the other seventeen pilots were dead or wounded or missing. I had been promoted to lead the flight.

As August staggered into its last week the damage was beginning to tell on both sides. Thirty-three major attacks were made, 23 of them directed against airfields and nerve centres of Fighter Command. In two weeks the Germans lost 373 planes to the British 277.

Those below watched eagerly, convinced that smoke flowing from an enemy aircraft heading for home would soon overcome the pilot and force him into the sea. Every Spitfire appeared to be executing a victory roll as it made its way back to base above cheers and hat-waving. Parachutes were a common sight and the target of any Home Guard that happened to be in the area. One German pilot now living in Canada remembers watching them from the air after baling out:

I was swinging down in my parachute in a tricky wind and bleeding from a head wound. I looked down and laughed uproariously at the antics of the British Home Guard down below. They had their eyes on me and were constantly falling in ditches as they ran this way and that.

Luftwaffe pilot Friedrich von Goetz was shot down by Spitfires over Dover when flying an ME-109:

It was exactly 10.23 a.m., because by some reflex action I looked at my watch when my chute opened. Spilling air from my chute, I managed to avoid a high-tension wire and hit the ground hard. The Home Guard quickly grabbed me. One gave me a cigarette, one began to bandage my head and the other started to strangle me.

All this time, there had been no raids on London itself. Hitler was quite content with Goering's attacks on British airfields. He wanted to guard against any action that would gain sympathy for his opponents in isolationist America – and he did not want to provoke retaliatory attacks on Berlin.

On the night of 24th August, fate intervened. Six German bomber pilots left their bases for a night raid on England. As the bomb-aimer in the leading plane crawled into position, he glanced down and watched the coast line of England slide slowly by. Ahead small puffs of anti-aircraft fire pricked the night sky.

A thick cloud cover over the target area left him and his colleagues staring into a soft white pillow. His fingers gripped the bomb release and his thumb slowly depressed the button to release his bombs on the outer edge of London, as he had been ordered. Unfortunately they landed in the centre of the city.

Churchill ordered immediate reprisals against Berlin.

One hundred British bombers headed for the German capital. Not surprisingly, a raid planned in such haste was not a success. Less than thirty of the bombers sent towards Berlin found the target.

In the following days Berlin was subjected to four more raids. Hitler promptly issued orders for a massive retaliation of raids on British cities. No longer would Goering be pointing at tiny airfields and fighter bases. He could aim at one of the largest targets in the world.

4

The First Raids

While he planned his attack on London, Goering decided that bombing raids on other cities would encourage Britain to surrender. A hundred and fifty-seven bombers took part in a series of night raids on Liverpool and Birkenhead and claimed that the raids had been concentrated and weighty. In fact the bombs had fallen over a large area and damage to the ports themselves was slight.

Mabel Speakman was one of eight children. Her father was a scrap metal merchant in Bootle, near Liverpool, and despite a handicap quickly set about protecting his home:

Dad had been in the First World War and had lost his leg over in France. He was considered to be a very fine air-raid warden.

Despite his wooden leg he could climb steps and step-ladders quicker than anyone else anyway and was a very conscientious man as far as his warden duties were concerned, not only of his business properties, but also the houses and the folk in them.

When the first air-raid warning was sounded we were in the act of putting up brown sticky paper on the windows. As a young girl it was only play-acting to me and I didn't realise just why I had to put it on the windows anyway in that particular pattern and could have thought of much more fanciful patterns to use. However, Mum ticked me off and said it had to go criss-crossed so that the glass would not fly over the room and the folk in the room when the bombs were coming down would not be hurt by glass splinters. (This proved untrue as we all got glass splinters as time went on.)

The future Mrs M. Clarke lived with her family in Liverpool. Their next door neighbour was a naturalised German whose children were born in Liverpool:

We used to have a sing-song to take our minds off the bombing, but for a few nights we heard this ticking noise. Dad told us to be quiet and we had to put our ears to the wall. Well, my Dad thought they were tick-tacking, as he called it, to the German planes overhead. So he mentioned it to a police sergeant.

He told his officer and the next night they all came round to our cellar. About six of them. They all put their ears against the wall. Yes, they could hear something. So they got a warrant and went next door. Was our Dad's face red. It was one of our neighbour's girls on a sewing machine . . .

Amy Crighton was living in Wallasey, near Liverpool:

There was just my husband and our two-year-old son. We had a little knitted hat for the boy and I stitched some pads to put over the ears so that he could sleep through the bombing. Going down the shelter was all routine for us. My husband's job would be to get dressed and grab the baby and I would take the baby's bottle and a candle . . . 'cause there was no lights or anything in the shelter. We would keep all the clothes and other things in the kitchen by the back door all ready to take each night. I always remember one night we went down and my husband had put his pants on back to front. We didn't used to wait for the warning. We just used to watch for the searchlights and when they came on my hubby would say, 'Ah, ah . . . get ready. We're going to get it tonight.'

One time in the early evening I decided to take the baby and go for a walk with my husband's sister. We went down to visit my auntie and the searchlights came on and the warning sounded and she said, 'Oh, you're not going to get home tonight.' They lived in a small two-up and two-down and used the brick shelter in the middle of the road. Anyway, we joined her for the night. Next morning we went back to the house and saw my husband. He'd been on the night shift and was on his bike looking for us. When we got home the door was off and all the army was in the house and garden and we weren't allowed in. A time bomb had fallen and was buried in the garden. Funny thing was the mailman had been and since he couldn't get in he'd thrown the letters up the hall and in that mail was my husband's call-up papers.

Doug Higgins and his family were the only ones in his street who had taken up the offer of an Anderson shelter. When the bombs began to fall on Merseyside, they suddenly found themselves with plenty of company:

Have you ever seen a whole road full of people trying to get into one air-raid shelter?

Then there was old Mr Brown across the road who liked his pint from the hotel up the hill. He came home one dark and moonless night. A bomb dropped and a belisha beacon chased him down the hill. Those little legs never went so fast in their life.

He fell into the shelter that night exhausted!

How to become a teetotaller overnight!

Florence Heaney (née Thompson) had been taken to the Royal Infirmary in Liverpool for an operation on her throat:

The night after my operation a land mine dropped behind the hospital. The two very high windows, one either side of the bed, blasted inwards — I was buried under iron frames, brick, woodwork and glass. The lights had failed. I was in a side ward, myself and one other patient, a much older woman, Miss Dees, whom they managed to get out. Sisters and nurses in tin helmets, carrying storm-lamps, were unable to cross the floor to help me, it was too dangerous. They sent for St John's Ambulance men.

Window frames, bricks and rubble were moved off my bed (those men were so wonderful — cheery and talking to me all the time), however, they were not able to lift me out with the bedclothes. The room was quite light, the sky through the gaping windows was bright with flares and flames.

The men tried to free me and to their astonishment I was pinned to the bed with long slivers of glass. Eventually I was lifted above the glass and placed on a stretcher. Would you believe I didn't have a scratch or a cut on me.

One man said to me, 'Jesus Christ, you have had a miracle rescue!'

In preparation for the attack on London, Goering also decided to destroy the fighter stations that would be called on to defend the capital.

Mrs F. C. Williams, who was living in Croydon, suddenly found herself grabbing everything she could and heading for the back garden:

One Sunday lunchtime in September, 1940, the largest bombing raid over Croydon took place. I rushed my daughter, eighteen months, and son, two and a half, into the Anderson shelter at the bottom of the garden. I rushed back to my kitchen, grabbed my hat and the roast leg of lamb and rushed back down the shelter.

One woman who had joined the ambulance service in 1939 as a voluntary driver was caught up in the Croydon bombings:

I was working in Croydon and began extra driving tuition after work. This was obligatory. We were given large old lorries or vans to practise with, which were very heavy and difficult. (I was given an old laundry van and sometimes needed two hands to get into bottom gear.) Eventually I was accepted as a trained ambulance driver in case of war.

3rd September came and we were sent to one of the twelve ambulance stations in the district . . .

As I had a day-time job I was given night duty two or three times a week. There was always a canteen open. We practised frequently to get familiar with the black-out, with masked lights and sometimes in gas-masks.

One of the worst hazards in Croydon then was the trams.

Sometimes we could overtake on the left and sometimes on the right, and of course no street lighting to see when passengers were getting off and on.

In 1940, during the phony war, I got married, and as was the rule then, had to leave my job. However, we were still living in Croydon and I continued regular duty at my station. Stretcher parties and cars were also at the station with us. Fairly soon, mercifully, our small blue ambulances were delivered to us. These were a joy to drive.

Each driver had to be accompanied by a girl attendant and drivers were not allowed to leave their wheel when out on a call. We watched and worried over Dunkirk. Then waited again. I think the first nearest raid was over Kenley. We heard it but were not involved. Then early in August bombs were dropped on the factory next to Croydon Airport at sunset.

I had just come off duty and from a bedroom window saw several planes come in very fast and low, then saw the 'black eggs' dropping. I shouted to my husband. We watched the smoke rising until it almost concealed the sunset. After about five minutes the sirens sounded, but of course the planes had long sped off. The factory had been working non-stop with girl staff, no warning had been given, and the results were indescribable. Some of the stretcher bearers and rescue men were physically ill. Later on I was always relieved that I was a driver and had to wait outside an incident until a casualty was brought out.

When raids took place after dark, the sense of danger increased. Pamela Fife remembers being on duty on the evening shift in the main control centre of the Croydon ARP:

The siren had not been sounded, we were quietly chatting and all but three of the girls in the report centre adjoining our room were either in the canteen or the rest room.

At 7.30 all the lights went out, indescribable noise, objects flying in all directions, choking dust, then a few seconds of complete and utter silence before cries for help could be heard. Our roof-spotter rang down to us and, although I don't remember, I was told that I answered him and when informed that he thought the police station opposite had been bombed I gave him the reply, that it was us!

The staircase down to the basement was blocked with debris, so we had to get out via the underground passage leading to the police station. The three girls in the control room were killed (if the siren had sounded the death toll would have been higher). Apparently a lone German plane had jettisoned just two bombs, one hitting us and the other the working men's club where there were a great many killed.

I had head and facial cuts (I still have the label which was tied to my jacket before I was taken to the first-aid post) and on arriving there I was horrified to hear a voice saying I would have to have my head shaved. I was being married two weeks later!

Patricia Brooks was eleven and lived near Croydon. They had a small room under the stairs which her mother was convinced was the safest place to be in an air-raid:

When the siren sounded my father called us from our beds, complete with blanket and pillow each to settle in for the night. An older sister, who had a small baby, would never respond and my father would keep shouting until she did, hugging the baby. We were all very dopey for lack of sleep and one night when this happened it had been ages before we realised that my sister was hugging and talking quietly to a pillow and Terry, her small son, was lying on the floor in the bedroom.

The future Mrs B. Famfield was evacuated to Brighton as a thirteen-year-old and returned to her home in Croydon in 1940. The first raid she witnessed was on Croydon Airport:

We were at the Davies Theatre watching a film when a bomb landed about six rows in front of us. Luckily it was an unexploded bomb. There was no panic, due mainly to some soldiers who were in the audience keeping everyone calm.

I used to visit an auntie with two small babies trying to run her life in London's dockland and the devastation was terrible. The rats had all been disturbed and were running along the clothes line in the kitchen where the nappies were drying.

Dowding was under increasing pressure to move his fighter force closer to the coastal area where the ships could be protected, although he knew his fighters needed the distance and time to climb to meet the German force.

Unaware of the success that the British were having with their radar, the Luftwaffe began sending lone aircraft out over the North Sea to gather weather information and take photographs of future target areas.

The dynamic Canadian industrialist, Lord Beaverbrook, was made Minister of Aircraft Production and given the task of rebuilding Britain's aircraft fleet. He set about his task with a vengeance, turning out Hurricanes and Spitfires at the rate of 500 a month, four times the number of Messerschmitt 109s the Germans were able to produce in the same period.

Although success buoyed the spirits, those actually doing the work were exhausted, and a concerned Ernest Bevin, Minister of Labour, reduced the working week to a maximum of sixty hours.

British and German forces alike were taking advantage of a respite to build up their strength. The all-out battle had yet to be declared.

The south coast was still the favourite route for most bombers and a holiday at Dover could result in injuries from German shelling that had begun on 21st August from newly acquired bases around Calais.

The sound of these guns, which could be heard quite clearly across the Channel, was the only noise coming out of Europe.

Volunteer policeman George Betts had just finished a twelve-hour shift in his home town of Dover:

When the Germans occupied France, the very first time we heard shelling was when a convoy of ships was passing Dover *en route* to London. We could see gigantic splashes amongst the ships and although none were hit and since we could not see any aircraft, we realised that the Germans were using their French batteries to shell the convoy.

It wasn't long before Dover itself began to suffer. Of course no warning could be given when the first shells fell. At night we could clearly see the flashes of the big guns and then we counted the seconds (I forget how many). We hoped that the shells didn't fall near us, especially on the beach pebbles that we knew would be like deadly shrapnel that would fly in all directions.

Bernard Tulett lived with his grandfather:

We were given a bed in an old wine vault where the local wine merchant stored his stock. Owing to this when we slept there we could smell the pungent wine and I shall never forget it.

Every evening, about four o'clock, my job was to carry the bundle of bedding to the shelter for my grandfather (only blankets, nothing fancy) and every morning I had to carry the bundles back home. I overslept one day and because the siren went off early in the day the shelter was opened up and I was still in the shelter. I had been locked in.

Mick Fitzgerald was hop-picking in Kent when a fighter plane came out of the sky with smoke trailing from its tail:

Myself and about three young lads jumped up across the railway line, across some more fields and as we were running towards the plane which was burning, I picked up a machine gun. It was hot and covered in oil. The lads said, 'Keep it as a souvenir.' I said no and threw it towards the plane.

The pilot parachuted down and went towards an orchard. The local policeman lived nearby. He was a very tall man. Six feet seven. He was on his bike and asked us where the pilot had dropped down. I pointed to where I had last seen him and he said, 'Let's go and have a look and see where he is.' We went over some fields and into the orchard and looked through the trees and we saw him standing by a tree with his parachute caught up in the tree. The policeman said, 'Come on, lad.' He put his hands in the air. He was a nice lad, blond. The policeman took a Very pistol from him and took him to his home and phoned the military. They came and took him away in an army car.

Many of those living along the south coast found themselves diving for cover as the bombs began to fall. Valerie Street recalls going to Portsmouth to visit her fiancé:

I was eighteen and engaged to a lieutenant in the Royal Marines and he had invited me down for a weekend in Portsmouth to be near him and to understand a little more about his work and the naval blitz there. Little did I know then that I would be caught in my first enemy blitz.

Bill had found me some digs with a landlady who was well known to the Marines as kind, clean and provided good wholesome food. I will call her Mrs Jones.

The first night there, Bill and I had just finished supper, when the tummy-tightening wail of the sirens sounded and Bill had to leave hurriedly to organise the manning of the in-shore based guns at the Marine base.

Within a few minutes the booming of heavy guns could be heard, followed by the crump of landing bombs. For a while the earth seemed to shake and tremble and the noise outside the house was quite deafening. To my surprise and consternation, Mrs Jones began to panic and started shouting and calling out to God to save us all. Her screams each time a bomb landed somewhere were frightening and, never having been in a blitz before, I felt an urge to get out of the house and take my chances where I could see what was going on, whatever dangers such a need encompassed.

Mrs Jones tried to drag me into the cupboard under the stairs, but I was very averse to such a claustrophobic atmosphere and I tried to tell her, above the noise from outside and her screams of panic from inside, that I was going to stand outside in the garden.

Grabbing a saucepan from the kitchen, I put it on my head as a protection from falling glass and debris and hurried outside and stood on the front porch.

A cacophony of sound and brilliant array of colours lit the sky all around me. I wondered with frightening awe what on earth was happening to Bill, as I heard the sickening thud and crump of falling bombs, coupled with the shrieks of terror emitted by Mrs Jones indoors.

Suddenly as I stood watching and listening there was an almighty explosion and glass from the two front rooms came flying out into the garden and the curtains billowed out completely in tatters. My heart stood still for a moment and I really thought I had gone deaf. With the now whimpering Mrs Jones indoors and the ever-increasing noise and bombs and bumps and wardens' whistles and shouts from up the road, I felt totally inadequate and helpless as to what to do, and my conscience told me to go back indoors to see if I could try to calm poor Mary Jones.

The sight of me with one of her saucepans on my head suddenly broke the awful tension and she started to laugh.

I went into the kitchen to make one of the endless cups of tea and sat for a few moments with Mrs Jones until she felt calmer and the noise outside lessened in intensity. The big naval guns continued to boom and whistles could be heard blasting away further up the road and from this hour of noise and ambulance bells and fire-fighters shouting directions, we eventually heard, thank God, the sound of the all clear.

After a couple of hours of waiting and wondering and worrying, Bill suddenly turned up. We threw ourselves into each other's arms with relief and happiness. Mrs Jones was so relieved to have a man in the house again.

I had already been into the sitting room and dining room to assess the damage done by that one tremendous explosion and was staggered to see how the curtains had been ripped practically to shreds and all the panes of glass broken and flung out into the garden.

Bill then told us what he had seen on his journey back to the house. Mrs Jones' house was one of twenty in a row along one side of the street and four houses away was an open field before the next row of houses stood. By some incredible act of good fortune, a bomb had landed in the middle of the field causing damage to all the windows but no house had actually been hit.

The following morning we went to see the huge crater in the field and marvelled at our miraculous escape. It was my first insight into the real horrors of war and needless to say, I hoped it would be my last, but that was before I joined the WAAF and experienced more horrors down in Plymouth.

It was 8.30 a.m. and a group of Spitfires chased the ME-109s out to sea. One of the planes was shot down into the sea by Pilot Officer Richard Hillary. The next day the young pilot officer was himself shot down into the sea and was badly burned when his Spitfire burst into flames.

That same day the Germans tried a new tactic, mixing the fighters in with the bombers. It seemed to work as once more the planes made successful raids on the airfields.

From 29th August to 7th September there were 33 major attacks. Communication centres and operation rooms were being battered to the ground, and although pilots were being transferred from Bomber Command and Fleet Air Arm the number of pilots available was slowly bleeding away.

Yet on the ground the population continued to stare towards the sky and watch fascinated as the swirling vapour-trails twisted and turned above their heads.

Leon Kay found the sight of high-flying aircraft a thing of beauty:

I was in the garden of our new Luton home with my foster mother (Auntie Sarr) when she exclaimed, 'Aren't they beautiful!', pointing to some silver-coloured planes flying high in the clear blue sky. A series of violent explosions followed and we discovered later that the planes were German.

Bombing by daylight continued.

Fighter Command had come a long way from the opening days of the Battle of Britain and was determined that the Luftwaffe should not repeat the successes they had enjoyed during the earlier attacks. Air Vice Marshal Park brought his squadrons forward to tackle an attack heading for London over Dover and Beachy Head. He was able to divert the bombers and force them to drop their bombs on Canterbury.

The summer was almost over and the weather was beginning to change. Constantly told that the British were almost out of planes, one German pilot on seeing a huge RAF formation remarked sarcastically, 'Here they come. The last fifty Spitfires.'

Sydney Stevens' mother had moved to Amersham, to the north west of London, and he and his father had pumped out the water that had accumulated in the bottom of their Anderson shelter close to Biggin Hill airfield in Kent. They were lying reading on their bunks:

I heard the stick of bombs falling. As they got louder I piled some of our bedding over my head so as to muffle it, although poor old Dad moved his head to the side and had a nasty bang on the head from the side of the shelter which bulged inward.

He didn't like the war after that and moved to Amersham.

The air-raid sirens had become so much a part of the British way of life that people went about their business pausing only to look into the clear blue skies that had become the twentieth-century battlefields.

Servicemen on leave could be seen everywhere and seemed to spend most of their time dancing; local halls and the large palais *alike were always full. Those girls not in uniform were dancing to relax after long hours spent 'doing their bit' in the wartime factories. 'If this is war,' one seventeen-year-old was heard to say, 'why am I enjoying it so much?'*

Sid Shilton was living at Walthamstow and decided to join the Auxiliary Fire Service:

I'll tell you why I joined. Two of my mates went to a fire station one night and said it was a real good night out. They give you some drills and a bit of instruction then we go out and have a few pints afterwards. So I said, 'Well, that sounds all right — I'll come up with you tomorrow.' We didn't get paid, but when we did our initial training we got issued with a uniform and all the rest of it, but otherwise there was no money in it. We used to go out occasionally with the regular firemen on their red machines to get some experience but we just went whenever we felt like it.

In pre-war Britain it had been customary for women to give up their jobs when they married. But once war was declared their labour was in great demand, as May Powell of Oldham, Lancashire, soon realised:

I found a job sewing and making babies' gas masks. Each stitch had to be perfect and when you finished the sewing you had to let the sewing needle finish in the last four stitches.

Most women at the factory (the poorer ones) had pawned their wedding rings and had replaced them with sixpenny ones from Woolworths.

My brother was manager for a pawnbroker's shop and he bought second hand jewellery that had come out of pledges —

so I took them to work and sold them to the ladies who wanted to replace their Woolworth ones.

After this job I went to a little fish and chip shop and people used to come into the shop selling their toffee or clothing coupons for a few shillings because they couldn't afford to use them.

When I became pregnant I was ordered to go to the Labour Exchange and was asked if I deliberately got pregnant so I would not have to go on to war work.

The women who remained at home were learning to use a stirrup-pump to put out small fires caused by incendiary bombs. This operation required a bath or a bucket, which meant that it was of little use to many of the poor, who had neither of these things. But for one thirteen-year-old living in Aberdeen, Scotland, it proved extremely useful:

I remember spending my time on a Saturday using the stirrup-pump to wash windows for extra cash.

Incendiary bombs were part of everyday life for many throughout the war. They were packed in 36s in a cylindrical container. One bomber could carry five containers, which opened at a predetermined height, spilling the contents over a wide area and causing considerable damage if left to burn.

A public information leaflet issued in 1939 explained how to remove an incendiary bomb by placing it on a shovel or in a steel helmet. Underlined was the instruction never *to place the bomb in water, as this would cause it to explode.*

Despite this warning, the incendiary bomb was the easiest type to deal with – certainly there was nothing the public could do about a high explosive bomb, other than putting as much space as possible between themselves and the device in the shortest possible time. The incendiary itself was about a foot long and three inches in diameter. The moment it struck the ground, the magnesium core threw off a glittering shower of white, molten splinters which spread over a radius of about ten feet. The spluttering lasted about a minute, then the bomb would glow and burn itself out within ten minutes.

On 7th September in the dockland area of London, many volunteers complete with armbands and steel helmets would remember the instructions they had read and be thankful that the bureaucrats had had the sense to explain that the important thing was to snuff the bomb out before it caught anything else on fire. A sand-bag or shovel of dirt could do the trick.

J. R. Miles remembers the bravery of his foreman:

That nice gentleman had to have his leg amputated, having tackled an incendiary bomb.

He put a music box inside his false leg. I think it played the bagpipes.

From his base in The Hague, Goering decided that the British had pulled most of their fighter force back from the forward fighter stations. He determined on an attack that would bring the few remaining Spitfires and Hurricanes back into combat against a vastly superior force.

The target would be London.

It was a major error of judgement that had a profound effect on the outcome of the war.

5

The Heroes Were Many

By turning their attack from the exhausted and battered Fighter Command operations rooms and command posts, the Germans gave the British time to recover. Just one more week of devastating attacks on the airfields would have left them too weak to defend London.

As it was, the first attack on London came on a warm Saturday afternoon in September.

George Gardiner was sitting in his garden reading when the warning went:

I didn't take too much notice as there had been many warnings during the Battle of Britain, but no bombs. After a while I became aware of the sound of many aircraft and, jumping up, saw a number of aircraft flying fairly low and in perfect V formation.

A couple of anti-aircraft shells burst some way from them and my mother came dashing out of the house and we both dove into the Anderson shelter.

After they had passed we came out and things seemed to go quiet again. (The planes had gone on three or four miles to the docks.) After a couple of hours the all clear went, so we had tea.

Living on a corner I was able to peer over the wall and look along the street. I saw what I thought were thunder clouds, but after a while I realised it was smoke. I went out and found that a plane had scattered a few incendiaries around on the journey to the docks and that the National Fire Service were putting out the fire in a house around the corner by the simple expedient of knocking a hole in the roof and putting the hose-pipe in, which I thought would do more damage than the fire.

Skeets Ogilvie was a Spitfire pilot at a fighter station in Middle Wallop, Hampshire, that was called upon to assist the overwhelmed London squadrons. It was his first combat mission:

They scrambled our squadron and the old controller was saying, 'There's a hundred plus coming in over Dungeness, then 150 plus coming in over Greenay' and after a while I heard the flight commander say, 'Tally Ho!' . . . God, my eyeballs were hanging out and I couldn't see a goddamn thing in the sky . . . I looked all around and still couldn't see any of them . . . and I'm thinking what's this hundred plus business and I can't see any of them. Then I heard, 'Okay, pretty boy, beam attack.' I was number four in my section and I followed the others and rolled over . . . I nearly pooped my pants . . . the whole German air force was just flying along two or three thousand feet below me. The air was just crawling with these planes with black crosses on them . . . Heinkels and Junkers . . . I'd never seen so many planes in my life

Down we went in an attack right through the middle of them, trying to decide which guy I was going to try to take a shot at . . . I went through so fast that I didn't have time to fire my guns . . . I thought, 'Holy cow, this is a great start to combat flying.' I pulled up on the outside and started climbing back up and got in a position to do an attack by myself. And two ME-109s drifted by just on the inside of me. I was just cold meat . . . they were so close I could see the pilots both looking inward, the other way . . . neither of them had seen me on their outside. So I came out the other side of them and jigged around, got into position as quick as I could, opened fire on the first one and Christ, I hit the second one . . . I didn't hit the first guy I was aiming at, at all. Anyway by now I'd finished all my ammunition and headed back to Middle Wallop and do you think I could find that airfield? . . . They all looked the same to me in that part of the world . . . I couldn't find it at all and my fuel was going down . . . so I thought, Oh God, what a first trip, a belly-landing in a field . . . back to Canada and the colonies for me.

I picked a nice flat-looking field and started into it, and just as I was coming up to it I saw goddamn aeroplanes around the sides of it, so I poured the coal on again, went round one more time, put my wheels down and flaps and it turned out to be Worthy Down. So I got down, climbed out and nonchalantly asked the boys to fill me up like a real big operator, got a line on where my station was and went home.

Meanwhile in the dockland area, ladders were reaching into the air, followed by climbing figures in blue who were soon silhouetted against the flames, directing channels of water into each impossible-to-control blaze. Ignoring the bombs and shrapnel that fell around them they continued throughout the day to stand alone, high on their isolated perches.

There were five fire stations within the city limits and the engines had been housed to allow them to reach most parts of London within a few minutes. Every fireman knew the narrowest back alleys and the location of every hydrant within his district. The heavy unit pumps could pump as much as a thousand gallons per minute and with the back-up of smaller pumps, usually towed by taxis, the London fire brigade was an army at the ready. It was about to face its greatest test.

Hidden in the smoke and drenched by the cascading water falling down to the streets below, firemen ignored the sounds from above. Soon, guided by the flames, hundreds of other German aircraft made their way up the Thames to join those who had gone before.

Ian Dick followed the trail of the incoming bombers:

They flew in a circle for mutual protection, with the occasional glint of sun on metal or perspex as a fighter dived into the ring, when one of the circle would slowly peel away streaming smoke and lazily dive to destruction. The bombers came back at night to take advantage of the flaming docks as an easy pin-point.

The ack-ack was in action, of course, but to conceal the desperate shortage of guns, they would fire a few rounds from their positions and then up hooks, rush to another spot and bang off a few more rounds.

Unfortunately a forty-millimetre Bofors gun would sometimes

Above: Gas-mask cases being sold in the street, just before the outbreak of war.

Left: Not even the ungainly masks were allowed to get in the way of a neighbourly chat over the garden gate!

Left: Posters were issued warning the public about the dangers of poison gas and announcing details of local gas-mask testing, fitting and repair sessions.

Below: A police car fitted with black-out dimmers and an air raid siren.

Above: An important black-out reminder at an air-raid warden's post in Dartford, Kent.

Below: Blacking out windows at Westminster Hospital, 1939.

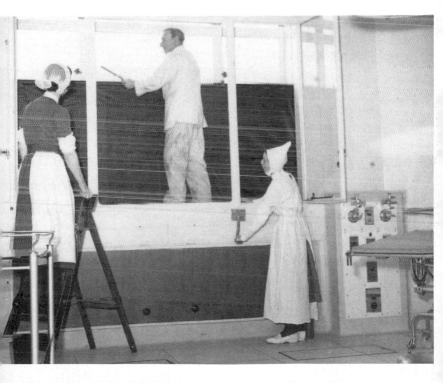

London Underground stations became places of both refuge and entertainment: above, people sleeping on the platform at Piccadilly, and below, a concert given by the ENSA (Entertainments National Services Association) at Aldwych.

Right: Many shelters, like this one, were built and shared by several neighbouring families, with an entrance from each garden.

Below: The hours spent in the shelters might have meant restless boredom—but not for these youngsters in London's East End.

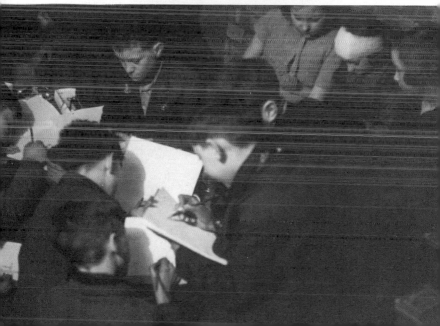

People found all sorts of activities to occupy their time in the shelters, from sewing to playing cards.

Shelters were sometimes brightly decorated for special occasions, such as this children's party in Greenwich, above, and an ENSA concert in Westminster, below.

Above: Many homes had their own air-raid shelters, sometimes in unexpected places—like this one, concealed among the cabbages at the bottom of the garden.

Left: A family in London's East End is taken in by neighbours after their home—visible across the road—has been bombed.

Above: The Anderson shelter saved many lives— everyone in this one escaped injury.

Below: Firemen tackle a blaze at a Bexleyheath shop after a daylight raid, 1940.

Right: In the shadow of a perilously tottering wall, rescue workers carry a young man from the debris of a house where he has been completely buried for twelve hours.

Below: A rescue squad helps to pull a casualty out of the ruins of her home.

Above: Local inhabitants inspect bomb damage in Gravesend, Kent, 1940.

Right: Sacred relics: a priest surveys the damage at Lamorbey Church in Sidcup, Kent, 1940.

Above: Smiles in the face of adversity: servicemen return home on leave to find their homes wrecked.

Right: A small boy carries an aluminium bath to the salvage dump in Chelsea.

Five hospitals were among the buildings hit during London's heaviest raid of 1941. Here, nurses clear up debris in the grounds and restore one of the damaged wards to order.

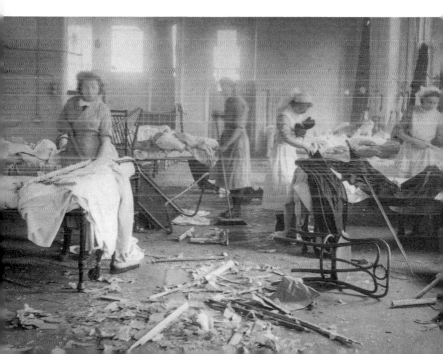

Above: Many buildings were reduced to uninhabitable shells, recognizable only by the wallpaper and the few hangings left on the interior walls.

Left: An injured woman is helped to a reception centre after her home has been bombed in a raid on Liverpool, May 1941.

Above: Salvaging treasured possessions from a bombed house, October 1940.

Right: The whole world — or what's left of it — in his hands: a boy holds up the remains of a globe that he has discovered in his bomb-damaged school in Northfleet, Kent.

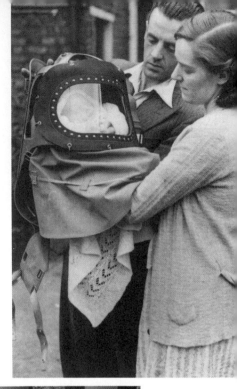

Right: The first baby born in London after the declaration of war arrives home wearing one of the new type of specially constructed gas-masks, September 1939.

Below: A mother demonstrates the newly invented gas-proof pram, December 1938. Made of wood, it incorporated a triplex glass window, an air-valve, a filter and a large bulb at the rear to pump out the air.

park outside the cottage, bang off a clip of shells before one of the gunners would knock on the door and beg a cup of tea. Alas, the vibration of their gun had usually shaken the cups off the shelf to smash on the floor, so they lost out.

K. James was seven and living in the East End of London the day the German bombers came up the Thames:

I had two playmates, twin boys, the Hardings, the same age as myself, who lived in Gainsborough Road, the next turning. We had played together that day when my mum called me in for tea. Not long afterwards the siren alert sounded and we went into our Anderson shelter in the garden.

Soon the sound of aircraft could be heard and my dad called me up to see a great mass of planes flying up the Thames. They seemed to darken the sky. Then the bombs started to fall. We crouched in the shelter which shook with each explosion.

Suddenly a tremendous bang was heard and Dad said, 'That's a near one' and after a while the all clear sounded.

We left the shelter to find windows broken in our house. A bomb had fallen in Gainsborough Road.

The bomb had made a direct hit on the shelter of my twin friends, killing them and the rest of the family. All but one elder brother who had been at a wedding in East Ham.

Sid Shilton was stationed at the fire station beside Liverpool Street Station, one of London's main termini:

On the first Saturday the docks were raided, I was riding one of the big red machines and we got a call to go to Doctor Barnardo's home in Stepney Way. 'Blimey,' I thought, 'I'm in fer a medal fer sure.' But when we got there all the kids had been evacuated and the place was empty.

As the day came slowly to an end sounds of the bombers faded, but the roar of the burning warehouses continued. The red glow from the docks competed with the setting sun; a great cylinder of black smoke curled its way skyward. But the day of carnage was not over: the bombers returned at eight o'clock. Throughout the long night the Luftwaffe crossed and recrossed the Channel in a slow, agonising procession as the people of London settled into the shelters for the night.

Esther Cutting recalls how she was making her way home from her job as a cashier in Woolwich when bombs began to fall:

It was quite unexpected because the warning didn't go until after the bombs had hit the ground. The next afternoon the docks were bombed for several hours. When that raid was over we could smell the burning and the sky was a huge red glow. It could be seen for miles that night and lit up the place like it was broad daylight.

Violet Regan and her husband lived in the East End of London:

The morning of 7th September was beautiful. The warm sun shone from a clear blue sky on to the little streets of Cubitt Town, Isle of Dogs.

No premonition of the terrible ordeal that was to be endured for the rest of that day and night occurred to me as I went about my usual chores. Of late the Luftwaffe had made quite a few hit-and-run daylight raids and when around midday the sirens blared their warning, I did not feel unduly disturbed.

My husband, who was a member of the Poplar heavy rescue service, was off duty and we were about to sit down to lunch, but on hearing more gunfire than usual we decided to go into the garden and stand for a while outside the Anderson shelter.

Very soon we heard the ominous drone of distant aeroplanes — German aeroplanes. The drone rapidly became a roar.

I remember the rising excitement of the neighbours as they anxiously called to each other. The frantic barking of the dogs — and my cat, which immediately sought the shelter of his own choosing. Suddenly, there they were. Silhouetted clearly against the blue of the sky. They consisted of three separate flights and they were heading in our direction.

They flew in what I can only describe as 'block' formation. Each section flying in straight lines — unlike the British 'V' formation. Altogether the three squadrons must have numbered over one hundred planes.

I watched in horror as bombs fell from the planes. My husband yelled at me to take cover, then he was gone, to join his colleagues at the heavy rescue depot in neighbouring Millwall. I helped to calm my terrified neighbour and her three little children who were screaming with fright and stayed with them until their parents arrived. Then I went into my own shelter.

For a long time I sat listening to the awful bedlam going on outside. To the explosion of bombs, clanging firebells. During short lulls I heard the crying of terrified children and the voices of agonised parents trying to soothe them. The barking of hysterical dogs went on and on. There seemed to be no let-up or respite from the awful din.

Later on I heard someone calling my name. It was our air-raid warden. He informed me that time bombs had fallen in the vicinity of a nearby oil-storage factory and the tanks were liable to blow up any minute. Everyone must leave their homes and take refuge in a school called the Glengall Road School.

I remember so vividly walking to that school carrying one of my neighbour's children wrapped in blankets. Great canopies of billowing smoke blotted out the sun and barrage balloons were falling down in flames. We were obliged to slap out sparks that alighted on us from all directions. More and more people were making for the school and as we walked through this nightmare we could hear the enemy planes above us diving with banshee shrieks to deliver their bomb-loads.

When we reached the school all of us, men, women and children, were herded into a long corridor which smelt dankly of damp cement.

I was terribly worried about my mother and father and it was with great relief I spotted them ahead of me in the crowd. After seeing my neighbour's family settling down, I at last managed to join my own family.

Everybody settled as comfortably as conditions would allow on the cold concrete floor, with the people facing each other with our backs against the rough surface of the wall. My parents sat opposite me and my sister and her three little ones made up the family group. The corridor was crowded in no time and was soon filled to capacity with scarce room to move. The bedlam outside never ceased.

At long last there came a lull from the bombing. With the coming of darkness the Luftwaffe resumed their attacks and all hell broke loose again. They added fuel to the already raging fires and started fresh ones.

It was terribly frightening to hear the fierce crackle of flames and constant crashing of falling masonry. Several times the huge building seemed to rock with the impact of high explosives. Gaping windows were all along the corridor and in my position I was sitting beneath them, facing the wall opposite. Fascinated, I watched the lurid reflection of the flames dancing on the wall. They lit up the corridor and bathed us in a baleful glow.

The menacing drone of the enemy bombers set already taut nerves on edge and somebody screamed, 'What's the matter with our guns? They haven't fired a shot!' It was quite true. Apart from the solitary salvo loosed at the beginning of the raid, no gun had fired a shot in our defence.

Thirst was worrying us. Very few had had any drink or food since morning — but for us, water was unobtainable — the mains had burst. I thanked God that my two little girls were safe in the countryside of Oxfordshire. Although sadly missed, they were spared this horror.

A fresh wave of planes made their appearance and it seemed they were heading for the school. We heard their engines low above us. Sticks of bombs whistled down and the air was literally torn apart in a loud rushing noise. Everyone instinctively crouched. The bombs exploded, rocking the great building to its foundations but by some miracle the school escaped unscathed and nobody was hurt. But the awful expectancy had been too much and I sensed a rising panic as the overwrought women burst into tears and the little ones, sensing their fear, began to scream.

Something had to be done and done quickly, so with parched throats a few of us tried to sing.

Then my old dad, possessor of a fine rich tenor voice, began to sing something they all knew, *Just a Song at Twilight*. It was touch and go at first as he tried to adjust his dry throat. There was a sudden hush as they listened to him sing, then here and there a few voices around us joined in, then more, and soon it became a swell as they sang the lovely old refrain with him.

What a tonic that was! To hear those tired folk lift up their voices in song, then more songs — and the wits among us with their spontaneous cockney humour had us all laughing in no time. But best of all the little mites were quietened and the badly frightened children had fallen asleep in their parents' arms, so the grown-ups too fell silent.

We must have all prayed for dawn, for blessed sleep had been denied us and it was such a long, long night.

When at last daylight came and the all clear finally sounded a gasp of sheer relief must have burst from one and all. In the cold light of morning we looked like scarecrows, smoke-begrimed and filthy; hair awry and clothing badly crumpled.

After sitting in one position for such a long time we ached in every limb and it was difficult to get the older people on to their feet. Very soon the wardens and special police appeared amongst us with their willing helping hands and warm comforting voices. 'Up's-a-daisy, Ma' and 'Come on, old soldier, show a leg there!'

Listening to them brought a lump to my throat because they were in a far worse state than we were.

Muriel Forster and Barbara Turner were professional dancers en route to the Queens Theatre, in the East End of London, by bus in the early evening of 7th September:

It was still broad daylight when our bus driver motioned us to look skyward where there was a dog-fight going on between Spitfires and German fighters. When we alighted from the bus we stood for a short while watching, not realising the danger that was to come.

On arrival at the theatre we had started to make up when we heard the sirens, so with great haste we rushed to the basement where we found several of our company of artists already there. We heard terrific bombing outside. My friend and I went to look outside the door and saw a man leaning over a balcony at a block of flats. I looked away for a second and the next minute the flats just seemed to fold up and the man disappeared.

We saw an incendiary bomb had dropped against our wall, so I rushed upstairs to get some water but in my haste found the large jug I had would not go into the sink, so could not fill it up. We dashed with it across the stage, with the scenery crashing down all around us, when a warden approached and ordered us to get all personnel and go into a new air-raid shelter outside our dressing-room, which eventually we did after long intervals to avoid shrapnel which was very heavy. Afterwards we learned that the shelter wasn't finished. The cement was still wet.

The all clear finally went, so we returned to our dressing-rooms to pack up our belongings as there would definitely be no performance that night. The telephone rang.

On answering it I was astonished to hear someone was wishing to book seats!

A. W. Wall and his wife were caught in a particularly heavy raid:

We decided to go by bus to see if my wife's mother was okay. She was, so we had a look around the City Road and saw where one church had been practically destroyed. But one wall with a large crucifix was resting on another building. However, the sirens went off and we dashed back to my mother-in-law's house in Chatham Avenue — a street of old-style buildings split up into blocks four storeys high. Each entrance was sand-bagged at the front and inside where the stairs commenced. In the block where we took shelter were about twenty or 24 people of various ages.

The raid got heavier and heavier — I felt tired, and a woman said, 'Go and lie down in my front room', which I did under the window. I don't know what time it happened, but there was a terrific crash and a blinding flash! A bomb had fallen through the front of a block opposite, across two storeys of our block and into some empty houses behind us. It blew me out of the window and into the street. There were screams from people, fires, dust and debris everywhere!

I climbed over the debris at the front of the block into the second lot of blown-up sand-bags and pulled the first person I saw out into the flame-lit street. This person was covered in dust and grit, as I was. The person was my wife! To think that of all those in there it was my wife I rescued — God was good!

I went in again and helped those who could move out. About six of us ran out into the street. One of the persons I was carrying asked me to put him down by a wall as his leg ached. I looked down. He had lost a foot.

Alf Cunnell, a national fire serviceman, was standing behind a fire-pump at the East India Docks as the fires danced and crackled their way through the countless empty warehouses. Suddenly he heard a voice calling from behind him:

A coal-lid in the middle of the road began to move and a man's voice called from the pavement.

'Has the all clear gone yet?'

'No, you fool, get back inside,' I called.

With that his head disappeared back down the hole and the cover of the coal-chute slid back in place.

Daylight finally arrived and with it the sound of the all clear. As the German bombers flew back towards the coast of France, they left behind a city of angry people, slowly emerging from their hiding places to see Britain's newest heroes, the blackened and dishevelled firemen who, though exhausted, continued to direct their hoses on the smouldering remains of ruined buildings.

Everyone knew that there was more to come. The following day, a Sunday, saw the streets of the East End of London crowded with people searching for relatives or gathering up bits and pieces of belongings scattered by the bombs the night before. Some were already making their way out of town, others were looking for the deepest hole in which to hide before dark. Many felt that the safest shelters would be found in the centre of the city, 'where the toffs lived'. With blankets and sandwiches they set off in family groups for the 'safer ground' of the West End.

Irene McCarthy remembers that on the Sunday night, her mother decided that she was going to take her family to the public shelter at the corner of the road to be with neighbours, rather than face another night of bombing with just her husband and daughter:

Early on Monday morning a bomb fell on the entrance to our shelter, blowing up an ARP vehicle and killing the crew. A neighbour standing in the doorway was also killed. We went to the back of the shelter and crawled out of the escape hatch. We eventually made our way to Watford later that day to stay with friends.

Dickins and Jones, a department store in Regent Street, became a favourite for so many seeking a deep shelter that police were called to take control of the crowd. They were quickly organised into a queue and by 7 p.m. the first 700 were allowed in to take shelter in the large basement. In the months to come many would queue for hours in the hopes of getting inside.

Irene Sullivan's father had a fruit and vegetable shop in Holloway Road, north London. The family were fortunate in having a Morrison table shelter in the home but nevertheless felt they needed something extra to protect them:

Dad piled one-hundredweight sacks of potatoes on top. We hated any kind of shelter but my mother was insistent.

We were in (or under) the shelter when we heard a bomb whistling down and a colossal bang — the ground seemed to come up at us. 'That's close,' said my father, and looked out on to the main road. Grey forms were running past the shop saying, 'It's around the corner, Guv!' My father rushed off, for my grandparents lived around the corner in Liverpool Road. It was a direct hit with one of the first thousand-pound bombs.

My granddad, step-grandmother and aunt were killed, but two relatives were rescued from under the piano.

It seemed as if fires had broken out all over the East End. The biggest was in Surrey Docks, where the heat was so great that paint on the fireboats blistered. Flaming pieces of wood were thrown into the sky and settled, starting other fires. As the warehouses caught fire, so did the goods inside. One contained rum and each exploding barrel threw burning liquor over the building.

The fire-fighters locked into battling dozens of fires were asked to keep a look-out for parachutes during the attack. Certainly the weather was right and with such a large number of aircraft attacking Britain, who was to say that England was not 'softened' for the long-awaited landings?

Photo reconnaissance had shown that the invasion ports along the French coast were filling up with Nazi shipping and four captured

German spies claimed that Hitler's preparations for the invasion were
now complete. Everyone agreed that Hitler needed to invade before the
winter, only a month or so away.

The code word for an 'imminent' invasion, 'Cromwell', was sent
around the country during the attack on London. Unfortunately many
could not remember whether 'Cromwell' meant to look out for an
invasion or that German troops had actually landed. In one location
army troops began blowing up bridges. In another the local Home Guard
rang church bells, signalling that the invasion had taken place. In small
villages strangers with foreign accents were looked on with suspicion
and on the coast all eyes were turned to the sea. But all that could be
seen coming from the east were bombers on their way to London.

In the first few days of the bombing, most Londoners stayed indoors
if they could. Those that did venture out found themselves embarrassed,
turning their heads from people scrambling over the rubble searching
for the prized bits and pieces that made their lives meaningful.

Yet these were the lucky ones. During the raid a thousand of their fellow Londoners had been killed. The German planes had dropped about
330 tons of high-explosive bombs and over one thousand incendiaries.
Smoke still rose above the river east of the City. Blackened and exhausted
firemen continued to direct their hoses on the smouldering embers as
police directed traffic from the potentially dangerous buildings and
barred the sightseers that had already begun to move in.

R. R. Bennett was fifteen when the war started. Living in south west
London, he had seen the slow build-up to the raids, first the daylight
attacks and then sounds of aircraft after dark.

In the second week of September he and his father looked to the night
sky and were surprised to find masses of parachute flares falling:

After a year of total black-out, the novelty of night light seemed
too good to miss. As I recall there was no bombing, no ack-ack fire,
just the sounds of aircraft droning to and fro across the locality.

A few days later, they were told by a passing air-raid warden that what
appeared to be a very large bomb had landed in a nearby cemetery:

It had reduced the superintendent's three-storey house to bungalow
status, but he and his family, all friends of mine, apart from being
shaken, bruised and scratched, were otherwise safe. An enormous
amount of superficial damage had been caused to surrounding
property. Our attention became focused on a large parachute hanging

on its shroud lines from the brick parapet of Clifford Bridge, adjacent to our house, which carried the South Circular Road over the Waterloo–Richmond railway lines. Our immediate reaction was, of course, that a parachutist had landed. Without any clear thought of what we were going to do, Dad and I went up on to the bridge to see what it was all about. We saw a large cylindrical canister propped against the parapet; and it was from this that the parachute was dangling.

More rumours of earlier in the day came to mind and my immediate thought was that the canister was a much-publicised container of arms, radios and other essentials for the rumoured spies, insurgents or whatever.

Both Dad and I thought we should at least see how to open the thing and find out just what the contents were. With only the reflected light from searchlights, it was not apparent quite how to do this. Dad, ever the keen DIY man, thought he might have some tools to aid our quest.

For my part, I was reluctant to do too much about it as by then I imagined that a Nazi spy cell disguised as nuns would emerge over the crest from the other side of the bridge, to claim their goodies.

All our speculation was suddenly brought to an end by the arrival on the scene of a local retired naval officer and eccentric. Although he had some undefined connections with the ARP, he was brandishing a sword and shouting foul imprecations about the rumoured Nazi hordes and what he intended to do to them. In the middle of all this a local bobby appeared as if by magic and managed to calm things down. He, it seemed, was fairly well 'clued up' about things that were dropped by German raiders and informed us all that the thing was a land mine and we should make ourselves scarce while he contacted his station to find out what he should do about it.

The Bennetts made their way back to their windowless home and joined the rest of their family. Soon an ARP warden advised them to evacuate the area. They went to stay with some friends of Mrs Bennett's:

The raid was intensifying and thoughts turned towards taking refuge in our hosts' Anderson shelter. This however was, as there were only two of them, of minimum size and could in no way hold the nine of us.

It was finally decided that at least the four children should be stowed away in the relative security that the shelter offered. No sooner was this done than the customary whoosh and ground-shaking thump heralded the arrival of a bomb nearby. It transpired that this had not exploded, so once again it was whistle and warden time. And 'evacuate the premises'.

Our hosts had relatives fairly close who they were sure could accommodate them, but not the again-dispossessed seven. After some discussion with such ARP personnel as could be found, the family were on the road again, this time heading for an emergency reception centre for refugees at Barnes Green.

This was some two to three miles distance, it was gone midnight and the raid was still worsening. I recall that at one stage during this trek I put my status-symbol steel helmet on the head of my youngest brother, who was still being trundled along in his pushchair. Only afterwards I wondered how he reacted to the weight of this, but at the time his safety seemed to be the priority, as shrapnel from exploding AA shells was bouncing off kerb stones. However, he reached maturity without rounded shoulders or a permanent stoop, so the weight of the helmet cannot have been too damaging to him.

When we arrived at the reception centre at Barnes it was full and we were told to go to the Odeon Cinema at the junction of Upper Richmond Road and Sheen Lane. After a two miles or so trudge back on our tracks we arrived and were admitted to the doubtful security of the cinema. Some hundreds of people were milling about in the aisles, but eventually order prevailed and we gratefully organised ourselves in some seats . . .

I can remember officials of various sorts made 'putting you in the picture' announcements from the stage. The best of these was that the film show for the current week would be screened. The feature film, as I remember, was *In The Nick Of Time*, the title of the second feature escapes me.

At what I suppose was just before 6 a.m., my father left us to go to work, he was on the six to two shift at Watney's brewery.

The all clear had been sounded a short while before, much to the relief of the captive audience of late-night cinema-goers. The film show had been quite well received, but it had been difficult to concentrate upon plots punctuated by earth tremors or the explosions of nearby bombs.

Our refugee status took an upward turn shortly after Dad had gone. Cups of hot steaming tea were dispensed and pies or pasties steaming hot from the local bakery were distributed among the masses.

The feeding of the 5,000 was never as good as this.

Esther Cutting remembers standing outside her house on the Sunday morning and watching as hundreds of people congregated at the local school, preparing to evacuate to a safe area:

It had been arranged that a fleet of buses would take them where they had to go. The people were mainly elderly or young women with their children.

The buses did not arrive, so it was arranged that the people would spend the night in the school. That night the school was heavily bombed and very few people got out alive.

After another night of heavy bombing a tired London returned to work on Monday morning. There were still fires raging unchecked and many of the collapsed buildings had uncounted bodies lying in them. Volunteers could be seen, dishevelled and covered with dust, picking and pulling in the debris. Police stood guard at the corner of many streets warning those attempting to enter of unexploded bombs waiting for the bomb-disposal units.

The bombing continued on the docks for four more days and nights. The familiar rows of terraced houses and warehouse buildings had been turned to rubble.

After a night in the cold brick shelters, many people could be seen settling down under railway arches, in warehouses and even church basements for more comfortable protection.

The first days of terror bombing forced many to leave their homes and look for safety out of the area. Flames and noise were everywhere and no sooner had the 'all clear' sounded than more bombers could be heard approaching.

As the raids continued, provision for the homeless became critical and rest centres quickly became overcrowded. Adding to the numbers of those who had been bombed out were many who had been forced to leave their homes because of the hundreds of unexploded bombs yet to be defused.

The bomb-disposal units were vastly undermanned and had received only the most basic of training.

Some people took the opportunity to loot shops and houses that had lost windows and doors. In between raids, children gathered pieces of shrapnel as souvenirs.

It was a few days after the first raids that the idea of using underground stations as shelters was born. Thousands of East Enders had taken temporary refuge there and refused to leave. It had been planned to use the stations for the injured and to transport troops, and London Transport officials and police tried to dissuade people from bedding down on the platforms. They found themselves overwhelmed by crowds who had bought tickets and then refused to leave the platform.

Within days, more than 150,000 people had settled in the deep tube stations.

When Marie Lewis came off night duty at her local railway station, she would go straight to Bethnal Green tube:

I would be so tired that I would lie down on the concrete platform and all around me were men, women and children sleeping. When the last tube trains came in, passengers stepped over the people lying there . . . rows and rows of them.

One Saturday there was almost continuous bombing for so many hours starting from the afternoon. The docks were set alight and even when darkness fell you could read a newspaper in the street from the glow of the fires. It was like Dante's Inferno!

Sometimes the bombing was so bad that ambulance men had to use sacks to pick up the pieces of bodies. No-one could say for sure that we would see the next day, yet we sang in the shelters.

My husband came home on leave, and the evening he came home we tried to make up for lost time. Suddenly, without warning, there was a terrific crash and our ceiling came down on us just as we were making love. To say the earth moved for us is an understatement!

Some, like Jean Mills, needed help to overcome their fear:

I was in such a state when we had the air-raids, I used to go to the shelter with a pot in one hand, I used to be so sick.

Millie Driscoll remembers the effect the bombing had on her family:

After tea on Saturday, 7th September, I had gone with my eldest sister to St George's Cathedral when the air-raid warning sounded. After a little while we left the cathedral and whilst walking down St George's Road home we could hear the noise of the planes and gunfire. I wanted to run but my sister said we would be all right and held my hand very tightly.

When we got to our house in Pastor Street, neither of us had a door key, all the family were in the Anderson shelter in the garden and could not hear us ringing the bell and knocking on the door. I was very frightened and crying. Eventually my father came up from the shelter to go to the toilet and heard us and opened the door. We went straight into the Anderson shelter which was very small, meant I think for six people, but there were ten of us in it. Later on, my father and a friend went into the house to get some refreshments for us. When they came back he told my mother that we would be lucky if we didn't get hit, as we were surrounded by fire.

I was sitting on a small folding stool in front of my sister with my head on her lap and I fell asleep. Suddenly I was awake and there was a lot of noise. Everybody was talking and my father was trying to get the door of the shelter open. When he did, we couldn't see the house, just a big cloud of dust. As it settled we realised that the house was still there, but badly blasted. The back window frame had come out and was blocking the shelter door. Then we heard whistles and the ARP men were running up and down the street, calling everyone out as the gas-pipes in the road had fractured and there was the danger of further explosions. As we walked into the house a candle on the kitchen table was still upright and burning, although all the windows had blown out and the doors were lying on the floor.

When we got into the street there was a big hole in the road and the gas leak was burning. We had to go to the public shelter under the big Burton's shop at the corner of St George's Road and London Road.

The sky was very bright and we just walked along with our neighbours. I don't think anyone ran.

The next day my father and a friend put up boards at the windows and tidied up as much as they could and fixed the street door on again. We had no water, only a stand-pipe about five or six houses up from ours on the pavement and no gas.

My poor mother had to cook for six of us each day on an open fire for twelve or fifteen weeks. (We didn't even have a fire with an oven at the side like some of our neighbours.)

The people in authority said we could continue living in the house, but we couldn't sleep there, it was too dangerous. So we slept in the public shelter until the Wednesday but it wasn't very deep. We could hear all the noise etc.

My father had been blown up three times in the First World War and the noise and no sleep was having a bad effect on him. Our doctor said he should get out of London or sleep in the underground, so from then on we slept down the tube. I would go across with my cousin about four o'clock with an old thick table cover and wait outside the entrance of the Northern Line tube station until the warning went, then run down the spiral emergency stairs on to the platform to claim our place between two chocolate machines. My mother would come as soon as she could with her and my bedding. My father and sisters would all arrive with their bundles and we slept on the platform.

My father and sisters would go home in time to get ready for work and my mother and I would wait for the all clear.

Every morning there was more damage and Dad would try to fix things before going to work and Mum would clear up the dust and soot that seemed to be everywhere.

Many, however, were determined not to be forced out of their homes. In future raids, it was estimated that 64% preferred their own beds to the shelters and only took cover when the bombs appeared to be dropping particularly close at hand.

Gordon Tothill was living in London . . .

. . . just where the Northern Line, the underground, came above ground . . . the railway track was half a block away. This was a favourite target. The Germans would come along and drop bombs all over the place. So the houses on our street were a bit of a mess. They had an air-raid shelter in the park but I wouldn't go down there. My mother threatened all kinds of things, but it was an awful place. There were just concrete benches along a wall that you were supposed to sleep on. They were so narrow I kept falling off. We tried taking these little lilo beds and blowing them up but they would go flat in the night, so you were back where you started. I tried it several times but it was no good. Anyway, the bombing got pretty bad and they had a mobile ack-ack gun that used to BOOM! BOOM! right outside our house and what with the searchlight at the end of the street my mother finally said, 'I've had enough of this, you're going into the park shelter and that's final.' So off we went to the park shelter.

Next morning when we came back home a bomb had fallen just a few doors down. There wasn't a window left in our house and the doors were all blown in and my bed was absolutely peppered with shafts of glass, with long pieces sticking out of the pillow. Eventually we got a Morrison shelter. I remember having the job of putting this together because with no Dad someone had to do it. I'd cut myself at school pretty bad and had one hand in a sling, so there I was working with my left hand lifting these huge pieces of metal to form a table shelter in the basement.

The sirens would go and we'd all climb under the table and into this. Eventually I'd find myself staying in bed despite all the shouts of my mother.

I'd go off to sleep again and you know, you can sleep through all kinds of things. But there was always something happening. Our air-raid warden was putting water on an incendiary bomb and it exploded. Took half his face off. I never did find out if he survived it or not. He was such a nice old fellow and real conscientious.

The numbers of people like 'the nice old fellow' who seemed to be in a position of authority grew as the raids increased. The need for drivers, ambulance workers, wardens and firemen was desperate and those who did come forward performed magnificently.

Mick Fitzgerald set off to join the ARP:

I had a Morris Isis car and when I reported to the council depot they said, 'Can we use your car, too?' I said, 'Yes' and they put four stretchers on the top of the car. We used to do 24 hours on and 24 hours off, all for three pound a week. We used to practise first aid on each other and that was all right at first, but when the real thing started that was a different story.

One night the bombs were falling all over the East End and we were kept very busy and just nearby was a block of flats. An air-raid alert was on and we could see a German plane flying in the sky. We never heard any bombs drop, but a man came running into the depot with a child in his arms all bleeding. The man was shouting 'For God's sake, help us. A bomb has dropped on the flats.' I said to three of my mates, 'Come on, let's go!', but the supervisor said, 'You can't go until you fill out an incident report.' I said, 'There are people up there who need our help.' So a couple of ARP blokes got in the car and we went to the flat.

It was about two o'clock in the morning and was very dark as I drove around the building. I was expecting to see rubble and bricks everywhere, but there was only a few bricks lying on the pavement.

We went into the flats and it was pitch dark and we heard somebody shouting for help. We went in and there it was. A bomb! It had gone through the first floor and straight through to the ground floor where the people were using it as a shelter. The women and kids were lying around the edges of the room and the men had been in the middle playing cards. The bomb had dropped right in the middle of them. It was chaos. They were all covered in bricks and rubble and were crying and groaning.

We started to dig them out. We dug a young fellow out and as I pulled him up by the armpits half his body came away. He was dead, so I dragged him outside and put him up against the wall. His eyes were wide open looking at the sky. I went back inside and helped pull a young girl out and she only had one leg and she kept crying and saying, 'My leg hurts!'

I was glad every night when my 24 hours were up and I could go down the tube for a sleep. I was called up in the army about a year later. I was glad to get in the army for a rest.

Bill Batt was sixteen and a messenger on a bike for the ARP in London:

One night in October 1940, I came off duty at midnight and started to cycle home. There was a raid on, the sky clear, full moon, searchlights, ack-ack firing away and fires burning some distance off. It was possible to read a newspaper unaided.

During a temporary lull I set off. In those days it was very difficult to obtain batteries for bicycle lamps, so as it was so bright I switched off my lights. Since the road was deserted, I rode along the wrong side of the road.

After a couple of hundred yards a voice shouted 'Stop!' and from under a tree appeared a policeman, properly dressed in his hat and wearing his gas-mask haversack on his chest. He called me over.

'Do you realise that you have no lights on your bicycle?' At that moment we heard a bomb falling; we fell flat on the ground. It landed some distance away. We got up. Dusted ourselves down.

He continued, 'And do you know you were riding on the wrong side of the road?' Another bomb whistled down and shell splinters were falling. We got up and for the next two minutes or so I was given a lecture on the correct way of riding a bike at night.

London's black taxis had been commandeered for the war effort and with a tow-bar affixed on the back to pull a small pump, had been deployed as back-up appliances to the main fire-fighting force throughout the capital.

With the main seats in the taxi taken up by ten fifty-foot lengths of canvas hose, the crew had to sit on the little square pull-down seats usually used for extra passengers.

Frank Tolliss and other members of his crew of the London Auxiliary Fire Service came from all walks of life:

They were mainly barrow boys from Camden Town and nearby Queens Crescent, but we also had stand-by actors, a cinema attendant, building plasterer and an accountant. A pretty mixed bunch of lads, but the barrow boys were the ones to see that we were comfortable and as well fed as necessary.

After a few weeks of standing by and no enemy action in London, the crews were moved into local schools which were made into temporary fire stations, the crews being split into three watches, red, blue and white, doing a term of duty, two days on and a rest day.

Kenneth Cass was an auxiliary fireman working for the Bath City Fire Brigade in the west of England:

During one of the big raids on Bristol we were sent over to help that city, this being common practice at the time. On arrival we were directed to the city centre, a part called Old Market where the Corn Exchange roof was on fire.

We worked all night on the roof and managed to save it. I remember on going down inside there was a nice marble staircase with offices on each landing. We stopped two floors down and tried one of the solid oak doors to see if anyone was trapped — the water we had been pouring on to the roof had collected inside, so when we got it open we were met with a wall of water several feet high which shot down the stairs, taking us with it.

By the time dawn was breaking and the noise of bombs and gunfire had almost ceased, I remember how cold it was — there were ice crystals all over our helmets. However, when we got down to street level, sheltering in a doorway was a night watchman or caretaker. He said, 'Here you are, boys' and produced a large bottle of whisky!

Never have I had a drink gone down so well . . . and I'm a teetotaller!

Most accounts of the work of firemen concern themselves with the large cities that were under attack. Richard Ford served as a country fireman with the Chipping Sodbury Fire Brigade. With the news of the possibility of a German invasion they were issued with a Boar War rifle with three rounds of ammunition to defend the fire station:

My duties, in the event of a fire or enemy air action, were to cycle round the houses of the off-duty firemen and recall them to duty and then to carry out such duties as may be required of me, either at the fire station or the scene of action. One of the most pleasant aspects of the job, greatly prized by me and greatly envied by my school friends, was that I used to be released from school for such duties.

The equipment of the regular fire brigade at the Chipping Sodbury Fire Station consisted of a Morris Tender, Humber car and two Drysdale 55 gallon per minute trailer pumps.

In the summer of 1940, the nearby city of Bristol, which was only twelve miles away, was a favourite target for the raiders. I well recall seeing a large flight of enemy aircraft passing over Chipping Sodbury one morning in bright sunlight. The white puffs of exploding anti-aircraft shells among them seemed to have little effect, but over Bristol itself our own fighters appeared and engaged the raiders with vigour and success, bringing down several enemy machines. Although interested in the dog-fights in the skies, I missed seeing them fully as I was busy tearing round on my bicycle, with bell ringing, furiously recalling firemen to duty.

Once during an air-raid alert four firemen were playing cards in the Chipping Sodbury fire station. Suddenly there came the whistling of a falling bomb and the four of them dived quickly for cover under the table. Then, just as quickly, one of them reappeared, grabbed his winnings from the top of the table and dived for cover again. The whole operation was completed before the bomb reached ground level and exploded not far away.

It is difficult to imagine a more dangerous job than that of the bomb-disposal crews. Major Ovens was posted to London in 1940:

In one early big raid we were called to assist in digging out some unfortunates, residents in a guest-house that had been hit. The bombs were whistling down and when one whistle seemed to be coming down on me I dropped to the ground and cowered in the gutter alongside the guest-house rubble. Lying face down with my steel helmet on the back of my head I felt a nudge in my back. I looked up and there I saw a diminutive ARP lass who said, 'What you want, luv? A nice hot cuppa?'

On one occasion I was dealing with a UXB (unexploded bomb) adjacent to a railway line and near a row of houses. The area had been evacuated pending the time when the bomb was made safe.

When the bomb had been exposed, all engaged personnel retired to a safe distance, while I prepared to defuse the bomb.

I was just about to descend the excavation to the bomb when I saw a movement nearby. I saw a chap peering over the garden fence. I asked him why he was not away at a safe distance like everyone else. He replied, 'I could see you were an officer, so I thought it can't be dangerous if there's an officer hanging around.' He had served in the First World War.

Another time I had successfully defused a UXB in the garden of a large house which was threatening a factory nearby. The bomb had penetrated fairly deeply, so we had to make a large excavation. The excavated material was piled alongside the digging.

When the all clear was given, the house owners were allowed to return to their homes. The owner of the house from whose garden we had taken the bomb watched it being loaded.

I was about to get on my motor bike to get to the next job when he approached me and, pointing to the excavation works, said, 'What about all that?' One of the sappers who overheard him said, 'Don't worry about that, guv. The bloke from Kew Gardens will be around to make it tidy and ask what plants you want to put in.'

Sergeant Waterhouse was sent to Bristol to join a bomb-disposal unit for four weeks:

My first night out in Bristol I went to a service canteen. A sergeant major stopped me, saying he wanted volunteers for fire-watching and I had just been accepted as a volunteer. On the roof three floors up an old man was sitting in a small hut. He informed me that a raid would take place in about five minutes. This proved correct. He told me to watch for fire bombs, 'over there,' he said. If I saw a fire bomb I was to rush with a scoop and sand-bucket.

Some time later I saw a bomb and ran into the black night and put the damn thing out. No further action. I stayed till dawn when, to my horror, I saw that I had run across a stone parapet about two feet wide. The building had gone some months ago.

One in ten bombs that fell on London didn't go off. Some were defective and others had a delayed time fuse set to explode any time. Not surprisingly, the Royal Engineers, who had to deal with them, were extremely short of personnel. Thousands of people made their way from their homes to the already crowded rest centres to wait until the bomb at the end of their street had been moved or defused. The most famous of these bombs was one that fell on the night of 12th September, 1940 and lodged itself close to the foundations of St Paul's Cathedral.

It was finally removed by the bomb-disposal squad and driven with great haste to Hackney Marshes where it was dealt with. The resulting explosion caused a crater one hundred feet in diameter.

Most people continued to work throughout the bombardment. The eight hours they could spend working beside friends helped them to take their minds away from what was happening outside.

The moment an air-raid alert was sounded, all employers were obliged to send their workers to the shelters or into the basements of the buildings. Many hours were lost through the alarm being sounded for a small raid that would have had little or no effect on the workers' safety.

So Churchill introduced the concept of 'roof spotters'. Only when the alarm was given by a spotter would the workers be sent to the shelters.

Alongside the volunteers who did important and often dangerous jobs were the 'regulars' whose experience in peace time now played a major role. The policeman on the beat appeared everywhere there was danger. People like Thomas Jones of Liverpool helped others with little thought for their own safety:

I arrived home one morning after a night duty of some fourteen or fifteen hours to find the street devastated. Home Guards were posted to keep out unauthorised persons. Shaking the ceiling off the bed, I took off my boots and climbed in and went to sleep. Some short time later, I was awakened by a Home Guard who insisted that I leave at once, the implication being that I was an undesirable in spite of my police uniform, albeit a rather grubby one. Using some language that a police officer should perhaps not use, I told him to go away. In between times I can remember standing watching a quarter of a mile of dock-side warehouses burn because there was no water and no fire engines if there had been.

After the fire burned itself out, the evacuated tenements at the rear presented a peculiar picture. The steel-casement windows hanging down bow-shaped with molten glass hanging like icicles. The bomb-disposal crew who dug out a bomb had just winched it above the ground when it exploded and wiped them all out.

John Davies was with the Auxiliary Ambulance Service in London:

The station received a direct hit one evening and was nearly totally destroyed. By a chance of fate the whole station had been evacuated to a school nearby in the morning because another thousand-pound bomb had landed in a garage opposite and had not exploded. In the confusion it was not realised that we had evacuated the station and we received a call at the school to proceed to the station to look for survivors — ourselves!

Joan Room (née Siobhan Kelly) had started her nursing career at Fulham Hospital in 1940:

On our way back we noticed a big formation of planes very high in the sky. It was a very lovely clear September afternoon, we were happy and the sight didn't cause us any disturbance. We went to tea in the dining room in the nurses' home and later to our rooms.

As dusk and then darkness fell, we prepared to go to our sleeping quarters, which were bunks in the tunnel leading from the main hospital to the nurses' home on the other side. We pulled our curtains — lights off of course — and it seemed as if the whole of London was on fire.

The bombing continued on through Sunday and on Monday morning a bomb fell on Fulham Hospital. The noise was deafening — dust and dirt were in the air — the smell of the explosion is something I shall never forget.

We dressed in our usual uniforms and went on duty although it was hours earlier than our normal 7.30 a.m. start. We were directed to prepare patients for immediate evacuation.

The water mains had burst as a result of the bombing, so we

were without water supply. I was given approximately one third of a cup of water and with the bib of my apron filled with cotton wool I was sent to swab clean the nose and mouth of each patient. (Washing was out of the question.) It still amazes me that there was no panic or sign of fear. We juniors acted as though everything was normal.

The only drinks available were undiluted fruit juices for staff and patients alike. The patients were soon on their way to other hospitals by bus, car and ambulance and we nurses were sent to search the rubble for anything we might find, false teeth, specs, photos etc.

As I went about my business, a photographer handed me a cat and asked me to stand for a photograph. I was too shy and gave the cat to another nurse close by. The next day the centre page of the *Daily Mail* showed two pictures, one of the bombed hospital, with headlines 'Another Hospital Bombed by the Huns' and 'Brave Nurses Rescue Hospital Cat'.

Florence Cunnington (née Mitchell) was a nurse in an emergency hospital in Hendon, north London, that was bombed three times:

First it hit the dispensary and destroyed most things there. Then it fell on one of the wards killing five children, two of whom belonged to one couple, and the next hit the lodge and destroyed the building.

I remember well the nights when the sirens went. We slept in the long air-raid shelter built for us, sisters in the first part, staff nurses further down and then came us probationers.

On going on duty one morning, one poor old gent said, 'You are a fine lot of nurses.' I said, 'Why?' and he said he was calling for the bed pan and a nurse crept out from under his bed.

Those working to relieve the pain of the injured in the streets continued to 'do their bit' regardless of the danger. Tom Bard was with a first-aid unit working in London during the heaviest of the raids:

An oil bomb sheared the foot off a man except for a small piece of skin on the heel. Blood was spurting freely when the first-aid party arrived and the leader immediately applied a tourniquet. He was then debating how to bandage the wound effectively because of the detached skin when an onlooker said that it should be cut off.

The first-aid man hesitated and the onlooker then produced a card which said he was a doctor and offered to do the job. This was accepted and done and the stump then bandaged by the leader and the victim laid on a stretcher under a blanket to wait the arrival of the ambulance.

On clearing up, the first-aid leader realised that he had a boot with foot in it to be disposed of. This was settled by putting it under the blanket and sending it to the hospital with the owner.

In a square near Bayswater a bomb dropped on a block of flats, slicing through the middle and leaving four floors either side visible from the street. The first-aid party waiting for the heavy rescue to do their bit were suddenly surprised to see a woman on the top floor of the left hand side sit up in bed. Despite the danger, one of the first-aid workers dashed into the building to bring her down. If she had got out of the bed on the left side she would have trod on nothing and landed four floors below. Instead she chose the right side, put on a pair of glasses and dressing-gown and walked through a door. The first-aid worker met her and helped her down.

We found her deaf and short-sighted, but she certainly got out the right side of the bed on this occasion.

A bomb dropped on Paddington Station and trapped a man behind a huge pile of debris. A small opening was formed — it could not be too large because of the danger of collapse — and the man was told to lie down, put his arms through the opening and be dragged through.

He was told to be perfectly still while this was being done because of the debris, but ignored the warning and twisted from side to side. Just as he came through the opening he continued twisting and drove a nail through the side of his head and died on the way to hospital.

We must have got rather callous after a time. Clearing up after an incident to make sure we had cleared the site of dead and wounded one of the party called out, 'Here's a pair of legs.' The rest dashed over. The finder held up a pair of doll's legs and said, 'I can't find the rest of the body.'

The heroes of the blitz were many. Life went on and new life made its appearance with the help of people like Dorothy Lowman:

I did my midwifery training in the height of wartime. This training was divided into two parts, the first six months in hospital with an examination afterwards, the second part of six months on the district.

I was already a State Registered Nurse. Both these six months were worked in the East End of London. It was a great experience. The Luftwaffe was concentrating on destroying the London docks. I was walking the streets of Bethnal Green, Hackney, Shoreditch, in fact I shared a council house in Shoreditch with four midwifery pupils and two midwifery sisters who were also officers in the Salvation Army.

The conditions under which some of those babies were delivered was appalling, but in a peculiar way, complications were rare.

Babies have a habit of making their presence known in the middle of the night. With the black-out it was not always easy to find the address. Some were just rooms, or one room suspended amongst the ruins of a building. Some were houses on long streets where many were devastated, where the descriptive word 'slums' could be applied. Plus the devastation of war damage.

It was usual when one was sent to a mother who had started labour to go in advance of the midwife, to prepare and stay with the expectant mother and to send for the midwife when the birth was imminent. On this occasion the house was small, the windows almost on the street with a narrow pavement separating. It was a young girl living with her mother. Mum had put a mattress on the floor in the small, cluttered-up back kitchen. The afore-mentioned Mum was a very stout lady, always wearing a pinafore which was once white and a pair of nearly black plimsolls with holes cut to give her bunions freedom.

Like all the other East Enders I found they had hearts of gold, beneath the sometimes grime. I had to kneel on the floor to see to the mother to be, which, after a time, was rather back-aching. The sirens went and almost immediately the street became full of people heading for the shelter. They all seemed to know what was happening on the back kitchen floor and as they passed they tapped the window and there were shouts for example of, 'How yer getting on, mate?'

'Mate' was progressing satisfactorily to the accompaniment of bombs whizzing through the air. I was grateful when the midwife arrived to be there at the actual delivery, as under the laws of delivery I was not qualified to do it on my own, although under such conditions a midwife did not always get there on time.

A lovely baby was produced and eventually mother and baby were settled on the mattress under the table and the midwife and myself found our way in the black-out and between the bombs back to the council house at Shoreditch.

Regardless of whether you had been up all night, you still had to do your round the next day, to bath previous babies, make the beds of the new mothers. I visited for fifteen days the mother and baby I described and there was always a cup of tea waiting for me. I never fancied this because of the state of the back kitchen. So I usually sent up a little prayer, 'Please God, let me drink it fast so that Gran doesn't know.'

One day I arrived early and Mum was still under the table and Gran was washing the tea cup. To my horror she first emptied the contents of the chamber pot into the sink, then washed my cup and dried it with the same dirty pinafore, using a corner of it. How could I refuse to drink? So a bigger prayer ascended and I managed it in one gulp.

As I said, the East Enders were wonderful people in those days and one felt no fear walking the streets at night alone.

Peggy Mason was living at the Elephant and Castle in London. She was 24 years old when she had a baby in nearby Guy's Hospital:

I was in Guy's Hospital when it was bombed (with my new baby). When those terrible raids were taking place, about ten to fifteen patients were put on a stretcher, all sitting up back to back, nobody could walk, and we were rushed underground by the wonderful doctors and nurses. The tiny, new-born babies were all put in a large chest of drawers. When we awoke there were literally hundreds of us, men, women all packed tightly together. We had to be sent home when Guy's was bombed. I remember one night six of us walking single file trying to cross the main road to get to a basement shelter.

Soon after Margaret Burgess's husband joined the RAF, she found that she was pregnant with their third child. Everything seemed to be going well until the blitz started:

On 17th October my labour pains started. I prayed for a quiet evening. Please God no bombing. At 7.30 that evening I tucked my two little girls into bed under the kitchen table (downstairs). The sirens sounded. It started. I could hear the swish of bombs overhead — I peeped out of the black-out and the sky was alight with gunfire. The bombs were falling nearer. I paced the floor. The windows shook. Doors banged — my children were scared. The midwife arrived. She had cycled three miles through the air-raid to get to me.

My baby, a girl, was born at 10 p.m. with the bombs falling all around us.

Leslie Jerman thought that Hitler did one good thing by bombing London:

He drove the bed bugs out of our house, they had no bodies to feed on. Just before the bombing had begun in September there was an alarm one night. We got up and went into the living room (we called it the kitchen).

We sat there with the black-out frames up at the windows, with only the dial light of the Cossor Radio to see by. We sat there silently. There was no sounds, no aircraft. Suddenly there was a distant rumbling. My mother said, 'Hark!' Someone spoke. 'Hark!' she said again, more urgently. 'There was that distant rumbling.' Then my young sister said, 'It's your stomach, Mum!' We made a pot of tea. Nothing else happened that night.

Edward Skinner, a London policeman, was standing on the corner of Trafalgar Square on Sunday 8th September:

It was about 11 a.m. The siren had sounded when overhead I saw a German plane being chased by two Hurricanes, one flew under the Dornier. The tail unit of the German plane was shot away and fell outside a Pimlico pub.

Two of the crew parachuted out and landed on the Oval cricket ground, Kennington. The main section crashed on the roof of Walker's the jewellers, then situated on the forecourt of Victoria Station. One Hurricane with Pilot Officer Holmes went out of control and he baled out and landed on a Chelsea roof.

According to the news reports, the Germans were chased around the Oval by local housewives with brooms.

The bomb load had already been dropped. One landed in the grounds of Buckingham Palace.

I booked off duty at 2 p.m. and had to pass Victoria Station on my way home to Lupus Street so was able to view the wreckage.

Although Edward Skinner reports that both RAF planes were Hurricanes one was in fact a Spitfire being flown by Skeets Ogilvie:

I had made an attack with my squadron and flown through what looked like the whole German airforce – a mass of German aircraft – and was on my way round to make another attack – was sort of on my own and as I pulled up to get in position I saw this one German guy, a Dornier 17, he must have been in trouble, lagging along behind the others. So I attacked him from the side. A gunner returned the fire, then it stopped. I went round for a second attack and the crew started bailing out. One of them came out of the aircraft and went just over the top of my head . . . I thought he was going to go right into the prop . . . scared the hell out of me.

Then when the crew bailed out the aircraft started twisting. It was an amazing sight. It just broke apart in the air. The tail floated away and the wings just snapped off . . . the main part was the part, I suppose, that landed on Victoria Station.

A week later the Air Ministry received a letter from Queen Wilhelmina who had been watching the action, congratulating Squadron Leader Ogilvie's group, the 109 fighter Squadron.

The news that a bomb had actually fallen in the grounds of Buckingham Palace was a reminder that the family living in that large house was the same as any other . . . well, almost.

The Queen later said that she was glad she had been bombed: 'It makes me feel we can look the East End in the face.'

Bad feeling among the East Enders had been growing steadily as the bombing appeared to be confined to poorer areas. Constantly on the look-out for a place to hide, they were not happy to hear about luxurious shelters beneath the 'posh' hotels and expensive shops. Moreover, the rich seemed to be living as well as they had during peace time.

To make matters worse, it was not uncommon to see wealthy groups making their way home from the theatres via the underground shelters, amusing themselves by observing how 'the other half' lived. But in the following months there was less time for such 'tours' as Germany extended its bombing over a much wider area of the city.

Harold Nicolson's diary entry for 17th September reads:

Everybody is worried about the feeling in the East End, where there is much bitterness. It is said that even the King and Queen were booed the other day when they visited the destroyed areas. Clem [Attlee, later Prime Minister] says that if only the Germans had the sense not to bomb west of London Bridge there might be a revolution in this country. As it is, they have smashed Bond Street and Park Lane and readjusted the balance.

For 76 consecutive nights, with the exception of 2nd November when the weather was too bad for flying, London continued to feel the full fury of the Luftwaffe.

6

Making the Best of Things

After the first week of heavy bombing, the people in those areas under attack began to adapt to a routine. Straight after supper they prepared their bedding and headed for the shelters. The major shelters soon became overcrowded. The Tilbury shelter, in the East End, was one of the worst. This massive goods yard under a railway station in Stepney suddenly had to house 15,000 people a night. They jammed themselves in head to toe and attempted to sleep on the cold concrete floors along with the rats and excrement. Despite the conditions, every afternoon there were huge queues waiting to get in.

When the doors finally opened, there was a mad scramble for the better spots, those furthest from the stench of the open buckets used as toilets.

It was the same in the tube stations. People were packing the platforms and when these were full, attempting to sleep on the stairs. Once the power had been turned off at 10.30 p.m. and the trains stopped running, many climbed down on to the rails and vanished into the tunnels to make a bed space for themselves. There was no sanitation or washing facilities on the platforms and people could be seen walking down the tunnels to find a private place to relieve themselves.

Seven-year-old Esme Temple was travelling by tube to visit her sister's future in-laws:

I cried to myself when I saw all the people sleeping on the platforms which were underground in the centre of London. There must have been people there in the mornings as well as afternoons, but somehow the impression left me with a choked, sad feeling. Many of the platforms were not wide and a white line was drawn for the people who had to sleep there. Men who did night work and slept during the day had to curl up and if their toes and legs were stretched over the white line the guard would come over with a long pole and shove the sleeping men's legs back over the white line.

Yet there was a sense of camaraderie as, face to face with a common problem, people attempted to make the most of things. From this background of below-the-ground living was born the legend of a remarkable person. Micky Davies was hunched of back and approximately four feet tall. Those who met him would never forget him. He made his home in a Stepney shelter that housed 10,000 in the most appalling and overcrowded conditions. An optician by trade, he had lost his tiny shop in an earlier raid. He was a natural organiser and soon brought order to a chaotic situation. He had divided the shelter into three groups, families, single men and single women.

But it would need an army of Mickies to sort out all the shelters and soon the committees that had been organised by each one pushed the government into action. Eventually bunks were built in the shelters and tubes, which improved living conditions greatly, and made it possible to bed down the children and sit quietly by as they went to sleep.

Six-year-old Elizabeth Le Blond (now Hodgkiss) found that most of her friends had been evacuated. The AFS took over her school, leaving just one classroom:

There were about six or seven of us with one teacher. When the air-raid sounded we all moved to sit cross-legged under the big table in the hall — and lessons continued as normal.

Those of us who were left in London became quite used to the routine of the early evening. For a while we sheltered in our own Anderson shelter, but then we found that everyone was 'going down the tube'. The children in siren-suits and mother carrying whatever she thought we might need: food, blankets, comics — anything in fact. There was no rush, no panic, just a stream of people making for the shelter where we children would find our friends and have a noisy game before settling down for the night.

The tube trains still ran, of course, and I remember we had to sleep on the platforms and there was a white painted line beyond which we were not allowed to lie. They still had to cope with passengers.

After the last train, of course, it got much better — and if we continued to go down the tube regularly (and were lucky) we could even be allocated a steel bunk. I did eventually get to sleep on one, but it wasn't very comfortable.

Tickets were issued to regulars in the shelters to reserve a particular bunk.

Evening classes were begun and it was not uncommon to find a group learning dress-making as a drama group close by rehearsed a play. With so many strangers being thrown together in the shelters, there was no lack of talent ready to help pass the hours. Joan Pickford (now Garrett) and her sisters were all under six:

We were all encouraged to sing in the shelters. My sister and I entered in a fancy dress. How they found the enthusiasm for this I don't know, but she was the 'mighty arm' and I was 'make do and mend'.

Flora Wood remembers living in Tottenham, north London:

Near us there was and still is a big park, half of which in those days was allotments. It was decided by the council to do away with these and construct a huge shelter, as we were such a thickly populated area.

On the day the shelter was opened, I think by the Mayor, it was a field day with a band and happy atmosphere and everybody rejoicing. It was either the day or night after, the shelter got a direct hit. They didn't even bother to dig them out, there were so many. We had a letter from the council asking us to watch for empty houses and if we hadn't seen the usual people around. This was the only way they knew who was down there.

There were few who would not have given anything for a white knight to rescue them from the danger. Johnny Johnson fitted the bill perfectly:

I was in London during the blitz. I had been spending the night in London and I had to get back to my unit, so in the early hours of the morning I had set out. I was obliged to walk down a rather long tube station where everybody was getting up in the morning. Now, I was a sergeant pilot and had just got my wings, but I had never flown an actual operational aircraft.

I suppose I was eighteen years old. All these people saw this laddie in blue with a pair of wings up and they all cheered. I had to walk down this platform with them all cheering and you can just imagine the effect that this had on a young man of eighteen to be cheered like this, like a hero by all these people who were suffering all sorts of things, and it was pretty heady stuff.

Florence Morgan (née Pond) was 22 when the blitz started and lived in the East End:

That first night we just sat in our Anderson shelters — so isolated. We couldn't hear any ground guns challenging them, although our fighters must have been up there like they were in the afternoon — but as Jerry came in wave after wave, it seemed all we could do was wait, hope and pray.

As the blitz developed into a routine, we then used to hear our mobile guns and this was a great consolation — even if, as we have since learned in recent years from TV accounts by ground gunners at the time, 'We hadn't a hope in h --- of hitting the planes but it boosted people's morale just hearing the guns' and believe me, so it did!

My mother took it badly, so I arranged for her to be evacuated to some friends at Datchet. My sister went with her and I stayed behind with my father.

Night after night in the Anderson shelter with virtually no sleep and having to cope with work each day was beginning to take its toll, so Dad and I decided we would go to the nearest tube station each night — at least at the tube you had a chance of getting some rest.

Our nearest tube was Bethnal Green — an unfinished station — work had been halted on it due to the war. Like this, people not only slept on the platform as in other tubes, but we also slept on the railway tracks as well — our regular place was right alongside the railway track into one part of the tunnel.

Our house was now damaged so much it was virtually uninhabitable (mainly through a bomb only a matter of a few houses away in our terraced street). Dad and I accepted mainly living from work to a place for eats and the tube for sleep. We used to keep our bundle of bedclothes for the tube at work. However we kept clean during the period amazes me.

At the time I was only engaged to my husband, who was in the RAF. His family sheltered all night in a local communal warehouse on the Isle of Dogs, which had been reinforced for the bombing and fitted with bunks. When he was home on leave, my father and I would also go to this shelter to enable us to all be together, but I never felt safe there. It was on the dock's edge and to me the water reflection made it a prime target. They used the top floor of this building to store the remains of some people's furniture that had been bombed out and we saw this all go up in smoke one night when incendiary bombs had set this all alight. We had to stand by then ready to leave in case they couldn't get the fire under control, and at the same time a land mine dropped close by.

I never felt safe in this warehouse shelter and I am sorry to say that my fears were confirmed when this shelter had a direct hit later — many people being killed and injured. Immediately I heard, I telephoned my husband (then fiancé) to give details of what I had found out. All his family, mother, father, two sisters and brother had been injured and a sister of nineteen was reported missing. There was no time for the official records of whereabouts of victims — they were just drafted to any available hospital. By the time I found out where they were it was late afternoon and as it was getting dark it was time for the blitz to start again, so I waited until my husband arrived home on compassionate leave next morning.

We went straight away to the disaster spot and my husband offered to dig, but they declined as the civil defence and rescue parties were experienced in this, but we found that his sister that was missing had actually been brought out on the night it happened. Dead.

The funeral of his sister, so young, I shall never forget. They draped a Union Jack over her coffin and she was buried in a communal grave, which must have been the only way then of coping with all the casualties everywhere at the time. But the most impressive sight was the long journey to the cemetery. She had worked for a large food company and the employees were there in all their white overalls and hats, lining part of the route each side of the road whilst the funeral passed.

Audrey Bown's father had a greengrocery business in south west London. She was thirteen and remembers going to the shelter every night under the premises of a United Dairies shop:

We went armed with rugs and my mother and I wore thick, navy serge trousers — the first time either of us had ever worn such garments. There we would sit upright on hard benches until the all clear next morning (there were too many people crammed in to lie down).

As one can imagine, the atmosphere became very, very foul by the end of the night and one day my parents decided we would spend the next night in an area under the stairs at our home. It was a big four-storey house with a substantial staircase and the night of Friday 13th September, 1940 found us in three deck-chairs, together with three members of the baker's family up the road whom we had invited to share our shelter.

There was an anti-aircraft placement on Clapham Common and the noise from that as well as bombs exploding in the vicinity was terrific. Some time during that night the bomb fell that was to change my life for ever. I believe it fell on the cosmetic factory, but I can only recall everything falling down around us. Miraculously the staircase held, but the only way to the street was through the shop, but that was in ruins with piles of broken glass everywhere. I remember my father pulling me through the glass, pieces of which were still falling around us, and into the street.

There it was absolute mayhem. Ack-ack guns going at full strength, yet more bombs exploding and the sky lit up with piercing searchlights. To add to the nightmare, horses were running amok from the nearby stables, but somehow we succeeded in reaching the nearby trap-door to the shelter under the United Dairies and Father hammered on it for us to be let in.

Eventually someone lifted the trap-door and my mother promptly fell down the perpendicular flight of steps to the shelter below. Subsequently we found she had fractures to her hands, but it was amazing she had no more serious injuries (she was, however, to become an invalid for the rest of her life). I was told that I passed out in the shelter but can only recall the horrible taste of some liquid in a beery glass which someone was forcing me to drink. I remember the great joy I felt because Dad had managed to rescue my tortoise and Persian cat. The cat had been trapped, unable to move, for several days but was uninjured. Instead of a tabby, however, it was white with bomb blast.

Margaret Hoyle remembers working in a London shop. Since the bombing made it impossible for her to get home during the evening raids, arrangements were made in the basement:

It was fitted out with two sections, male and female — incorporating the fire-watchers and fire-fighters and the staff who couldn't get home.

There was a kitchen and a rota amongst the girls for cooking breakfast. In the evening a crowd of us would link arms and go out into the black-out to Marble Arch for our meal at Lyons' Corner House. The sirens always went at 6.30 p.m. and several times on our return we had to lie flat on the pavement up against the shops during a raid, being thankful to get back to the dormitory with its rows of hospital beds.

It was all great fun until the night of intense bombing and incendiaries on Oxford Street when John Lewis's store was ablaze from end to end.

When we emerged in the early morning to view the extensive damage, it was still burning. Our back entrance went out into Harley Street and hanging across the corner of a building was a parachute with its land mine dangling over the edge.

After that I decided to join the ATS and became a radar operator on heavy ack-ack gun sites, so felt I was doing my bit to fight back.

A. Gabe was a member of the ambulance service who was called to a shelter in south London:

The entrance was in the Borough High Street and was sand-bagged, fairly wide and once inside, a gradual incline to a flight of wooden planking stairs. I think my mate and I counted 120. Dim electric lighting, terrible stench of dank, cold air and quite a few hundred people, men, women, children, babies in arms, but the air was so heavy that when the patient on the stretcher or a chair was carried to the top, one was covered in perspiration and really gasping for air. Of course, we were offered help and were only too glad to get it.

They used to call it 'the deep shelter' and it really was.

Joyce Mason lived in south east London in a downstairs flat. They stayed in the kitchen, diving under the table when they heard a string of bombs:

I well remember one evening putting the saucepan on the stove full of milk and when we emerged finding it full of soot. When it was bedtime we — my mother, husband when home, the lady who lived upstairs who used to come down, and the elderly gentleman she looked after who was extremely deaf so wouldn't take any notice of the raids — we put a wardrobe slantingly in a corner and put a bucket behind it to make a little privacy for the toilet.

Jane Webber (now Fabb) was just four years old when the war started:

In the weeks prior to the outbreak of war, our next-door-but-one neighbours, Mr and Mrs Turner, had dug an air-raid shelter in their garden. My mother told me that everyone laughed at them — until the air-raids started, when the Turners generously welcomed neighbours into their shelter. It was standing room only and my mother said that, after a few nights, she couldn't cope any more and went back to her bed despite the raids.

We five children from our terrace (including the Turners' two) always had bunks to sleep on in the shelter. I can remember Mrs Turner bringing us bowls of dry cornflakes in the morning — I suppose there was no milk or sugar.

I had a Donald Duck gas-mask, as did Maureen next door, but I soon grew out of it and had to have an ordinary black one that wasn't so nice. Baby Barbara next door was put bodily into hers. A mobile gas-mask-testing unit came to the park and we went in with our gas-masks on to see if they worked: they did.

There was an ARP post in the park — a little stone building, great to bounce balls against. I understand in retrospect that much hanky-panky went on at night — well, I suppose grown-ups had to liven up the war somehow.

One day my mother had queued for hours to buy a piece of liver for dinner. As she was cooking it on a summer's evening with the kitchen door open to the garden, waves of German bombers came over. She later said, 'I thought — my liver or my life?' She chose the liver. She sent me and Dad to the neighbours' shelter and followed later with the liver, plus bits of ceiling plaster which had fallen into it when the bombs fell.

Later on the family next door to us 'shored up' a room in their house which was supposed to be safe. The mother and daughter soon evacuated from London, leaving Mr Mayston. Mum, Dad and I used to sleep in there, in the 'shored up' room with Mr Mayston. I had the indignity of sleeping in a cot (at the age of five or six) as there wasn't room for my bed. My father was the chief fire watcher for our road (he was too old for the Second World War, having served in the first), so was out most nights.

It always amuses me that my mother and Mr Mayston 'slept together' unchaperoned (except by me, of course) and always addressed each other as 'Mr Mayston' and 'Mrs Webber' as was the custom in those days.

I was never afraid of bombs as my mother did a great job in showing me no fear. However, I was terrified of guns, even our own anti-aircraft ones. There was a gap between houses opposite our house and one day, Mum was on the phone and I was playing in our front room when a German plane dived through the gap, machine-gunning. We could see the pilot's face. Mum dropped the phone, grabbed me and threw me into the cupboard under the stairs. I could hear the bullets rattling down the roof: that frightened me. We were also machine-gunned one day as we were out shopping — Mum pulled me into Sainsbury's where I was pushed under the marble counter.

Later in the war a friend's daughter, Felicity, came to stay with us. By now we had a Morrison shelter. My grandmother also lived with us much of the time and the five of us — Mum, Dad, Grandmother, Felicity and I — had to lie 'sideways on' in order to get in, so we couldn't put the fourth 'cadre' side to the shelter. In later years I realised that the adults' feet must have stuck out and I asked my mother how they managed. 'When we heard a bang, we pulled our legs up,' she said.

Felicity and I always thought the knobs on the side of the shelter (which were to fix the mesh side on) were custom-made for hanging up Christmas stockings and I wondered where we would hang them when the war was over.

Whenever we blew our birthday candles or stirred the Christmas pudding (made from I-know-not-what in those days of food shortage), the wish was always for peace. We had no idea what that was, in practice, but it was evidently highly desirable.

During periods without air-raids we had to sleep upstairs in beds and this wasn't so much fun, especially as Felicity and I were in different rooms. So as we said goodnight we added, 'Hope there's an air-raid' and my mother used to wince.

Ronald Showell was a River Thames waterman and lighterman.

We had an Anderson shelter in the back yard and my late brother, who was on leave from the RAF, dug a hole about two feet deep and set it in. If the blitz had started a year earlier we would have had trench feet as it had at least a foot of water in most of the time, till the council sent round some men who concreted them. Ours needed a chimney as our father would smoke. It was bloody awful. I stopped going down then.

I was in the scullery having a wash when the bombs fell. My father called out, 'Are you all right?' 'Yes,' I replied. It must have been close, so I slipped on my coat and went into the street. Not till then did I realise that two bombs had fallen. I called out, 'Anybody hurt?' At number 62 I heard a voice saying, 'I can't get out.' The lady was in the loo. That and the scullery was all that was left of the lady's house. Once I and a neighbour cleared away some bricks she came out. 'Thank you, young man,' she said. 'That was a bit close for words.'

Jean Emmins remembers there was an Anderson shelter in her garden in London that six used: her family of four plus two lodgers.

The bottom half of the shelter was underground, the rounded roof covered us and at ground level there was a dirt ledge. Father used to lay boards across from ledge to ledge and the first ones down there lay on the ground and the remaining boards were then put into place once they were inside. The latecomers then lay down on a mattress and sat comfortably playing cards by candlelight before settling down for the night.

Even now the thought of me lying there completely enclosed in a three-berth coffin with a foot of head room still gives me cold shudders!

May Powell had a choice of going to the shelter or continuing to work:

Being on 'peace' work, I always kept on working.

Vicky Tunbridge recalls that she loved to sing, which was not good for her mother's nerves:

As people got used to the raids they became less inclined to use the shelter — all except my mother. She was always off like a shot as soon as that siren sounded. In fact once, when I was singing away in the bath, she suddenly dashed out, off to her place in the shelter.

So much for my rendition of *Down In The Valley*. She thought the part where I sang 'Valley so low-ow-ow' was the siren starting up. I was trying to emulate the Andrews Sisters.

John Copley remembers a remarkable woman named Miss Loring in the East End:

She was elderly and unmistakably a lady in every way. A spinster daughter of a clergyman who had devoted her whole life to assisting the needy in Bow in the 1930s.

One wild night, her house, together with everything she owned in the world, vanished utterly. My mother met her later that day. She was, as always, immaculate and apparently quite unconcerned.

'Oh, those were nothing, my dear,' she said. 'They're just material things. The only thing I'll miss is my little dog.' Her dog still lay somewhere among the rubble.

Every night she'd conduct impromptu prayer meetings in the make-shift shelters, mere earthen-walled trenches with roofs. She did so that night, too. After the usual prayers she startled the congregation by adding:

'And now, let us pray for the Germans; that they may soon see the error of their ways before disaster overtakes them.'

There were mutterings and cold stares. Many of those present had become destitute and homeless the previous night, too. Prayers for the Germans were not uppermost in most of their minds. Probably not one other person in all of Bow could have persuaded at least some of them to remain on their knees and pray for the enemy, but somehow she did.

They don't make 'em like Miss Loring any more; come to think of it, they didn't make too many like her even then.

Margaret Spencer remembers working for Lloyd's of London at the age of eighteen:

Once the blitz started we were bombed out of the first two premises, using boxes for chairs with borrowed office equipment, typewriter etc, in temporary accommodation, until permanent offices could be found in the Lloyd's building. You can imagine the shock on finding, twice, a small heap of rubble where yesterday's offices existed. A rope with notice attached indicated our next move. (Incidentally, as women had never been allowed to work in Lloyd's hitherto, all female employees were required to be robed from neck to toe in dark overalls before setting foot in the hallowed underwriters' room.)

At the start of the bombing, all Lloyd's staff were instructed to go down into its deep and vast underground shelter at each alert. This refuge was a city within a city — once in, we were sealed off completely, the object being that life could be sustained for several days, if necessary, should the building collapse. It was a very eerie sensation to be so far down into the ground and I would have preferred to have taken my chances up aloft.

However, this exercise was too time-wasting as air-raids increased hourly/daily. We continued thereafter working on all floors with our fingers crossed! Lloyd's remained one of the few buildings intact throughout the blitz.

Making every lunch hour count, we'd often crunch down rubble-strewn Cheapside just to make sure dear St Paul's still stood and to listen to wonderful readings by many of the day's leading thespians from its steps — a fantastic boost to City morale. We attended lunchtime services in whatever City church was still functioning, albeit most of them in part ruins, and enjoyed piano recitals in the Mansion House by top concert pianists, including Moura Lympany.

My most poignant memory was of traffic halting at short intervals whilst rescue teams excavated and listened for signs of life after a Mansion House underground bomb had trapped hundreds of citizens sheltering overnight; at each whistle blast, even City workers seemed to freeze into silence, hoping and praying for survivors.

Searching for a place to put an Anderson shelter could be a problem. Daisy Howell recalls that her father decided to make use of a small piece of ground that backed on to Bow Road underground at the rear of their house:

My father dug a tunnel that was very deep down and put the shelter in between two old oak trees and the top of the shelter was level with the ground. So we were really deep underground, which saved our lives, my mother, my father and myself.

The bombers used to follow the blue flashes of the underground trains from up the line until they disappeared into Bow Road station. We always heard the bombs whistling down as soon as the trains disappeared into the tunnel.

A bomb dropped just the other side of the railway from us and when we came out of the shelter in the morning there were all kinds of things hanging in the trees. Clothes, sheets, bedding, eiderdowns and in our garden someone's wardrobe, handbags, coats, stage costumes. All the things belonging to the houses that had been hit came over the railway lines with the blast and landed in our gardens. My father went over to Bow Road police station, which was opposite, and they came down the street to help gather things up which were then taken to the police station in case the people who they belonged to were all right and could collect their belongings.

Jo Walters had arranged to go into an Anderson shelter with a friend a few doors away:

I ran up the road to my friend's place (she had children) and my mother-in-law (a large stout woman) would go into my shelter. But, alas, as we heard the bang of bombs and saw lights from molotov cocktails falling in our street, there was the funniest thing to see. We had a wire-haired terrier called Peggy and my ma-in-law was stuck in the entrance to the shelter, the dog under her arm barking away and her alarm clock ringing in the other hand.

Violet Podger (now Shilling) was twelve and with her fourteen-year-old sister made her way to a brick air-raid shelter:

My mother was expecting a baby so my father made a shelter for her and my two brothers, eleven and nine, in a chalk-pit at the bottom of our garden. So each night we would all go to our separate shelter.

When my sister and I woke up one morning we were informed that my mother had gone into hospital in the night to have her baby.

I went with my sister to tell my dad and he came back to our house, leaving my two brothers in the shelter. The air-raids in those days would start as soon as it got dark and the all clear would sound as soon as it got light.

We went indoors and not long afterwards I heard an aeroplane, so I said to my dad, 'Hark. Here comes a Jerry.' With that he went out to the garden to find my sister. The next thing I remember was the windows rattling and I had all the debris over me. I couldn't move and I could hear people trying to get me out. I was calling out, 'Help! I am here. Here's my arm. Can you see it?'

I was rescued and taken to the local hospital where I received treatment for shock and a slight concussion. I was kept in hospital about a week and kept wondering why no-one came to see me, especially my dad. Then at the end of the week my dad's sister came to see me. She was all in black.

She told me that my dad had been killed, and my sister.

My mum had a daughter the same day.

Doreen Barnley lived in St John's Wood, London. She had run home through the falling shrapnel:

I had worked that day until late afternoon. I was fourteen years old. My sixteen-year-old brother had gone to the pictures 'around the corner'. Three families shared the house. Relations of ours, an aunt and her niece at the top. (They were already in the Anderson shelter in the garden.) The Anderson was damp, small, so we left it to them to use. The family of four in the middle flat used to join us in our living room in the basement.

My brother came home early as he could hear the racket outside the cinema, and the family of four (the Everetts) joined us in the basement.

When we heard the stick of bombs fall, we all dived under a large strong table which had been ideal for a large family to eat at and now just the job to get under for some safety.

We got well and truly blasted — houses in the back (one where we last lived) got a direct hit, as did houses at the side of us. I was clutching my dog and facing the fire-place, which was only used part of the day. So I got the full force of soot over myself and dog.

My father herded all us women out to the Anderson shelter where we squeezed in. I had to stand bent over (I was five feet ten) all night still holding my little dog, who usually fought my aunt's dog, but they behaved well that night — aware of the crisis, no doubt.

I cursed the Jerries and wished one would land in my garden so that I could make him a nice cup of tea laced with cyanide.

Kathleen Heavens had an early warning system:

If a bomb was dropping near, our parrot used to turn upside down on her perch yelling 'Ohh!' When we saw her do that we all used to dive for cover under the big double bed.

Peggy Carter (now Gillingham) found a new method of tackling the incendiary bomb:

We had spent much time racing up and down the stairs of the old houses putting out minor fires before they got a hold. A shout from my mother told me that the garage at the bottom of our garden was alight. A quick dash to where an incendiary bomb had dropped against the garage doors which were well ablaze. I picked up the nearby bucket and tipped it over the fire.

To my amazement it went out like a light. Next morning I was surprised to find I had put out the fire and extinguished the bomb with a bucket of horse manure destined for the roses.

Fred MacLannan had his wedding reception in his sister-in-law's flat during the blitz:

We had forty people there. The ARP wardens kept coming round to pull the curtains because of the light.

All they really wanted was a free drink.

In the days that followed, despite being robbed of sleep by the nocturnal bombers, London continued to make the 'best of things'. Some, like Mary Offord, did the best they could without steel helmets:

Night after night we would head for the Anderson shelter. We all carried a pillow which we placed over our heads every time a bomb dropped.

Hundreds continued to watch the spectacle overhead as searchlights brightened the moonlit sky. Many who were forced to walk home when they were unable to get transport constantly looked back in the hopes of seeing one of the many taxis that continued to operate despite the danger. Whenever one was without a fare it appeared by magic at one of the many tea-wagons that stood at major junctions and served their customers regardless of what was happening up above. Even the buses continued to operate and only stopped to allow passengers to take cover if the bombing appeared to be getting particularly heavy. Henry Jackson was with Associated Press and was on his way by bus to his office when an air-raid warning sounded:

The bus conductor took a mouth organ from his pocket and marched the passengers off the bus to a nearby shelter, leading the way with renditions of *Tipperary* and *Pack Up Your Troubles In Your Old Kit Bag*.

Harold Nicolson's diary describes walking through a deserted section of London during a raid without a tin hat:

When things get very hot, I crouch in a doorway. In one of them I find a prostitute. 'I have been drinking,' she says. 'I am frightened. Please take care of me.' Poor little troll.

Some were caught outside when the sirens sounded their warnings. Brenda Skinner (now Dewar) was three and had been shopping with her mother. They had just got off a bus and were on their way home.

There was the most awful whistling sound. Mum said in a voice of panic, 'I didn't hear the siren!'

She pushed me under a clump of bushes growing in the grassy front of a crescent-shaped row of maisonettes. I saw the iced buns bought for teatime roll on the grass as Mum dropped on top of me to protect me from the blast of the bomb we had heard whistling. I remember an almighty BOOM! The ground shook under me and it felt like the sky had fallen. Mum lay so still. Then our rent collector came from the maisonettes in the crescent and took us to a big cupboard under the stairs. There he and his wife sat Mum in a chair and wrapped Mum's head in a huge white table-cloth. It didn't stay white for long as the scarlet blood soon showed through.

It seems the bomb fell in our back garden and the explosion wrecked our maisonette and blasted tiles from the roof of the church opposite. One of these tiles had hit Mum on the back of the head as she lay protecting me.

In King Edward's Hospital, where they took Mum, the corridors were full of people waiting for those who had been injured or were waiting to be cleaned and patched up. So many people needed attention that screens had been put up in the corridors to use as dressing rooms.

Having only grazed my knee, I was my usual nosey-parker self. My fourteen-year-old sister and Dad were forever dragging me back to where they were waiting news of Mum.

Dad took me to my Aunt Ethel in Perivale to sleep. Something woke me in the night and when I opened my eyes there was a faint glow in the room from the open door. I saw Dad silhouetted in the glow and as he leaned heavily against the door he said to me, 'Mummy is an angel now. I've just heard God calling her up to heaven.'

Mum died on 14th January, 1941.

Edna Meade (now Beeson) was sitting with her mother and sister in the house when they heard a deafening noise:

We had refused an Anderson shelter (they were dark, damp and often water-logged). I said we had better get under the table and rose to do so when the living-room door flew off its hinges and hit me on the posterior, thus hastening my action.

The rest is somewhat hazy as the lights went out and clouds of dust and plaster from the ceiling descended. I did notice however afterwards that the glass of the windows crashed in towards the bomb, which must have been suction from the blast. All food and crockery that was not broken was covered by a thick layer of dust so that even a cup of tea was out of the question. In any case, the water was temporarily cut off.

My uncle, who lived thirty yards up the road, was an air-raid warden and came to see if we were all right. My aunt had been in her shelter in the garden, which undoubtedly saved her life, as her house was demolished, as were about ten other houses. Five people were killed, four of them were two married couples and their dog which was in the garden shelter which received a direct hit. We were told that not a shred of any of them was found. The fifth was the father of five children, a milkman. There had not been room for him in the shelter, so he left his wife and children there and stayed in the house by himself.

My uncle brought over to us the eldest girl, a girl of about thirteen, and asked us to look after her while they looked for her father. She said to us in distress, 'My Daddy is in the house but there's no house there.'

Stella Woodham recalls living in a tenement flat in London:

A 'molotov cocktail' bomb set fire to the building. A lady sleeping in the second floor was fast asleep and was rescued by a fireman who found treacle around the bed. She had hoarded bags of sugar under her bed. The only casualty was a fireman who had been struck by a falling beam. I was seventeen and he thought I was his daughter so I sat and held his hand as the ambulance was a long time coming.

John Dawkins was five or six and living in London during the blitz. His father had built an air-raid shelter at the end of the garden, but for some reason they were unable to get to it before the bombs started falling:

I remember my Aunt Mollie saying, 'That bloody Hitler again' and being told off for swearing in front of the children, although at the time I thought that 'Hitler' was the swear word. Anyway, the siren had sounded (too late) and my cousin Kenny, who was older and a bit of a comedian, rushed over to Aunt's sewing machine and in mock horror pulled the wooden cover over his head. All this time bombs were seemingly dropping just down the road. Nobody was over duly bothered, we had a more immediate crisis on our hands. My cousin Kenny's head was stuck in the sewing-machine cover. His ears were the problem. I remember my Uncle Lester trying to free him, only to have his efforts rewarded by cries of anguish as the ears became further entrenched. After that everyone had to go and free the entrapped Kenneth; it became a sort of party game.

Nan Eaton had just said goodbye to her twelve-year-old daughter, who was being evacuated. As she headed home, she wondered about how to fill her empty hours. She finally found a job and ended up working seven days a week. She was living, with her husband, in a tall Victorian house in London when the bombing started:

My husband wanted me to go down the tube to shelter every night. I didn't have to sleep on the platform, as there was a private room used by the station master. I was there when the West End caught on fire.

In the morning, all trains and buses had stopped. I had to get to work somehow. We never thought of not going, even if we had been awake all night. After sheltering all night we still had to come out and face the daylight raids. I made my way to Marble Arch in the hopes of getting an 88 bus to work. I went through the arch and watched some men roping off a bomb with red flags when someone shouted. A man jumped on my back and pushed me down and shielded me from the blast. He had his jacket sleeve ripped off and I had a miraculous escape. Covered in rubble, my hands, chin, knees, nose and forehead raw and bleeding.

I saw in a flash a horse and cart going up in the air. A man on a bicycle and the men roping off the bomb all lying in the road — I think they were all dead.

The man who had helped me looked ruefully at his jacket sleeve, asked if I was okay and went off and never told me his name. I have often wondered who he was and if he survived it all.

I was now shaking with shock and worried because I had no more stockings. I could see an 88 bus coming and I ran for it as fast as my now shaking legs could carry me. On the bus was a man I worked with. He was shocked at the state I was in and advised me to go home and make some tea and he would tell them at work. We always had a roll-call every morning and anyone not answering was presumed bombed out or dead.

When I got home I had no front door. It had been blown off.

After this we decided to move into a little house in the next road, with a cellar.

Sunday mornings were spent on a bomb-site at the bottom of our road, being taught by real firemen how to put out fires in houses. They erected a shed and piled old furniture in it, then set it alight. We had to stand in line and pass buckets of water to put it out. All this in between trying to cook dinner.

The effects of the bombing would live with some forever. Anne Knight (now Varney) lived in Ealing, west London:

I was eleven years old, my sister Violet was twelve, my sister Pat was thirteen and Betty was nearly fifteen.

We had all been happily in the dining room of our house; the siren had sounded, but we were thoroughly blacked out and used to the routine of bombing. Mother was a stickler for discipline, so at 7 p.m., my sister Violet and I got ready for bed.

We slept in what we termed the breakfast room, which was on the opposite side of the front door, almost a twin to the dining room. Like millions of others, we slept on a make-shift bed on the floor.

Our house was only two years old, detached, right on top of the hill with a reservoir at the back of the house and a wonderful view across Harrow-on-the-Hill. It was a clear night, but rain was about. Being the baby of the family and Violet being the second youngest, it was customary for Mother to come in and see we were settled comfortably in our 'beds', kiss us goodnight and say God bless.

Violet and I heard the plane come over and got under the covers. Unfortunately Mother was on her way out of the dining-room door and caught the whole blast as the bomb dropped. She was killed instantly, injured as she died in the most appalling way with shrapnel.

My sister Pat had a shattered right arm — we did not know the state of anyone in the dining room. Violet and I calmly picked our way out of the debris, completely free of any injury. I can still remember the warm water under our feet due to the radiators being damaged; yes, we had solid fuel central heating, which was quite a luxury in those days.

There was no screaming. We got out of the front door, met up with Pat at the front door, also our maid, Jose. I have no idea who suggested it, but we walked from the house into Hillcrest Road and knocked at the door of what we called the reservoir cottage, where we were taken in. Pat's arm was in the most appalling mess, blood everywhere.

We were given a cup of tea and eventually Pat was taken away and people my parents knew gave shelter to Violet and me, also our maid.

My father at that time was on duty as a post warden. Of course he did not know it was his house that had been hit. Bombing was just called 'an incident'. Because of the situation of our house, it was customary for us to have two wardens outside our house, the idea being that they could telephone the post from our house should the need arise. On the fateful night both wardens were killed. One of the sad aspects was that Mother said that the wife and children of any warden on duty at our house could stay with us for company. On the night of the bomb one of the wives, with her small daughter, called Fiona, who was about seven, was staying. Fiona was already in bed at the back of the house in our lounge, but her mother was with the main body of the family in the dining room. She had shrapnel wounds in her back.

The wife of the other warden, who was called Mr Robinson, had a baby and toddler. They were not staying that night.

My sister Betty, whom we were never to see again, was in King Edward's Hospital, Ealing, and lived until Wednesday; no hope of recovery. Grandmother was got out unharmed and lived on for a few years.

The thing that I remember was how calm Violet and I were. We must have heard whispers that Mother was dead and that Betty was injured. We were made to stay in bed the day after the bombing. A doctor came to see us and the following day the doctor told us Mother was dead. We had a short visit from my father. He had always featured as a person who had authority and we simply did as we were told.

Each time there is an anniversary we do tend to relive the night our lives were changed in such a drastic way. Not only the trauma of the bomb, but the trauma of from that day, no mother, and in a way, no father other than as a figure of authority. The memory of the moon which appeared through the clouds as we walked from the appalling catastrophe.

The mists of autumn were drawing in and the short winter days saw the families heading for the shelters earlier each evening. The sounds of the throbbing bombers overhead began to tick away a longer night.

On 15th October, as on every night since the first of the September raids, the sirens wailed their warning that bombers were heading for London.

Those living in the vicinity of the Balham tube in south London gathered their bedding and headed for the deep shelter. At eight o'clock a screaming high explosive made a direct hit on the road crossing the station below. The ground shook and then began to sink as the explosion opened up a huge crater above one end of the platform. A mountain of earth and water poured down, blocking the passage that led to the exit. Slowly the filth and slime began to fill the underground shelter as the men, women and children fought to get above the rapidly-flooding cavern.

Sixty-four died that night in the Balham tube disaster. Never again would those making their nightly home in the stations feel completely safe. That night across London more than 400 people were killed and almost 900 seriously injured.

The continuing onslaught seemed to harden the feelings of those on the receiving end. Edie Swash remembers her mother giving her an assignment:

There was a chap down the end of the street that sold boiled beef and pease pudding and one day my mum said to me, 'Go down there and throw stones at his window, he's a German.'

Joy Hacking was 18 and found that getting to work was the major problem:

As the bombing intensified, it became harder and harder to reach the office each day. We did our best, sometimes taking longer to do the journeys than we spent at the office and travelling on all kinds of unlikely vehicles, including flat-top lorries.

The Germans had the habit of dropping high-explosive bombs on the railway lines, which meant that the trains drove as far as the crater, all the passengers got out and either walked or were ferried by bus to the other side of it and completed the journey in another train. Much the same thing used to happen with the trams and only the buses were able to find ways round the gaps. Parachute land mines were another hazard; the areas around New Cross seemed to be a favourite target and a great deal of devastation was caused there by them.

On at least one occasion an unexploded mine got caught up in the telegraph wires near New Cross station, which caused even more chaos for the commuters. It was safely dealt with by the bomb-disposal unit.

A plane dropped a stick of bombs outside the house of Joan McConachie (née Condy). One fifteen-gallon oil bomb fell on the roof:

I looked out of the shelter, saw flames going sky high and we all ran down the garden to see what we could do. Inside the house there was glass everywhere — all the windows were gone. My father ran upstairs, went up in the loft, grabbing a pail he filled it with water from our cold-water tank and threw the water into the fire in the bedroom. The roof had gone and where the oil had splattered on the walls there were dozens of little fires starting.

One policeman who was passing came in to help and gradually they put the fire out. The feather eiderdown was alight and we threw that out of the window. An ARP warden who was coming to help us yelled that he was covered in feathers.

In all our misery there were some things to laugh at.

Mary Birch's wedding day was not the perfect day that she had planned:

The morning was so quiet – no sirens! no bombs! — until an hour before I was supposed to leave for the church. Then the sirens. Spent an hour in the air-raid shelter in the garden.

Arrived at the church, so did ten other people — out of 78 guests, only those few could make it. No wedding took place because the registrar didn't arrive. We waited and waited because without that person no marriage could take place — not in the Roman Catholic church, it didn't.

We went to the hotel — the proprietor was delighted to see us — so pleased that somebody had turned up, even though we were not married. The photographer was invited to join us in the reception, bringing the number to thirteen.

During the evening many friends and relatives called to wish us luck, to drink our health and to say farewell (some had been bombed out, had lost their homes, everything. All their possessions gone forever. They were all leaving London.) Some decided to stay with us for the night and depart the following morning. (The proprietor had suggested that we stay in his cellar so that we could enjoy ourselves.) This we did.

Two days later my father went to the Registry Office, collected the registrar and brought him to the church. I was married in my honeymoon suit — needless to say there was no honeymoon!

Paulina Atkinson was visiting friends in Aldgate:

Not wanting to use Aldgate Station, a bus inspector walked me to Moor Street Station. On the way we heard a bomb screaming down. I put my head inside his overcoat till the bomb exploded. We then continued on our way.

A bomb could come at the most awkward of times, as Elise Love found out:

One night it was very bad and I wanted to spend a penny, so best place seemed to be with the coal. Just getting comfortable when a bomb dropped outside.

When I surfaced my knickers were filled with coal dust.

Patricia Poyser remembers being in a London hospital for six months suffering from typhoid:

I was four or five at the time. My father, who was serving in the army, tells me of coming in to visit me and finding other children and myself in the hospital corridor with potties on our heads as helmets.

Joan Murton remembers working as a junior in an engineering company when she was fourteen:

My dear old dad felt the cold, so he slept in my mother's old moth-eaten fur coat. I had five brothers in the forces who came home when they could at all hours and when my dad opened the door to them in the fur coat they nicknamed him 'Lord Rothschild'.

Enid Joyce Godsiff (née Brown) continued to shop in Oxford Street and remembers a large display of fur coats in the window of John Lewis's:

That night the raids were very extensive and most of the city was bombed. I arrived next morning to find that most of the roads were closed and firemen and ARP were everywhere.

Going into Oxford Street, John Lewis's was a smouldering mass and firemen were still fighting the fire. Among the debris and water were the fur coats. Most of them were wrapped around the hoses, others in the wet road. One fine man said, 'Would you like a fur coat, lady?'

After a delayed action bomb fell in their area, Bill Batt and his family lived with friends for three weeks:

At the time I was trying to learn to smoke a pipe but was not allowed to do so. The obvious place to avoid being seen was to go back home, climb over the garden fence, into the kitchen and sit down and smoke.

Awareness of the danger started at a very young age, as Dorothy Cobb remembers:

For part of the blitz we were joined at home by my older brother and his wife and younger son, John, then two years and nine months old. John got used to the sound of the sirens and when they sounded each evening it was a race between him and our dog Scamp to see who got to the cellar stairs first, John shouting, 'Cellar me! Cellar me!'

Hitler and Goering were coming to realise that London would not be easily brought to her knees. So the Luftwaffe began to expand its area of attack. First the provinces became the target of many of the heavy raids, then cities outside the capital began to hear the sounds of the approaching bombers.

A heavy raid on Birmingham was successful enough to prompt the planning of another attack. Although the Midlands had experienced earlier raids, nothing would compare with the three days of hell that were about to begin.

7

Coventry

On Thursday 14th November, a report from the Air Ministry reached Churchill. Intelligence had found that the Luftwaffe was about to launch its biggest attack of the war. Under the code name Moonlight Sonata, the whole of the long-range German bomber force was to be employed in a massive raid on an unidentified British city.

In the middle of the afternoon, Churchill, about to leave London for the country, was handed a note. Intelligence had discovered the name of the city. The might of the Luftwaffe was to be directed against Coventry. Churchill immediately ordered his driver to return to Downing Street.

Coventry was an important industrial centre in the Midlands, and for months it had been the target of random raiders keen to disrupt production in a number of factories vital to the British war effort.

At 7 p.m. on 14th November, the first bombers crossed the target area and began to release their bombs. Joyce Hampson (née Whelan) remembers it vividly:

All the 'old 'uns' kept telling us 'youngsters' (I was eighteen) that Jerry would never find Coventry. 'You see, we live in a hollow (demonstrating this with their hands held in a 'V' shape), we're right at the bottom.' As no one had ever been at a higher altitude than the cathedral spire we couldn't debunk this theory.

The first warnings came in July–August 1940. I can't remember the exact dates. Nothing happened, just the sound of an aircraft at odd times, which we were told was a Junkers 88. We got to know the sound very well.

Activity in the area quickened as everyone started to erect shelters. As there weren't enough to go round, we shared with the neighbours. All the men and women would help to dig the holes to erect the shelters in.

We were sharing ours with a neighbour and friend named Templeman whose back gate was opposite ours. 'Temp' was crippled with arthritis and used a wheelchair, but could manage to get into the garden. She had refused to be evacuated, saying that 'bloody Hitler wasn't scaring her'.

The fire-fighters used to help 'Temp' to the shelter. She would painfully make her way along, holding the garden fence and they would lift her down into the shelter.

One night the bombs got very close and everyone nagged her to evacuate as she was risking the lives of the fire-fighters who were men with young families.

Reluctantly she agreed to go next day and her daughter Kath went with her to relatives in Macclesfield.

By now the bombing had reached our area and my mother and my two young sisters left Coventry and joined 'Temp' in Macclesfield. Just after this we had an incendiary bomb through the roof of the house.

The resulting fire caused much damage before it could be dowsed, so afterwards we could only use the downstairs rooms, throwing mattresses on the floor to sleep on.

We were all so tired with this constant lack of sleep, we were getting some daylight raids too. You never knew when to expect a warning apart from the regular night-time one. It had been the practice in Coventry that when the clock struck 8 a.m., the factory gates would be slammed shut. Any worker arriving a minute late would be locked out and consequently lose a half-day's pay. We could go into work after the midday dinner break, same procedure then at 1.30. So lots of people were oversleeping through sheer exhaustion. Eventually these rules were dropped and we could go into work at any time, so at least the raids did us some good as the practice was never resumed.

Came the night of 14th November. A date stamped on every old Coventrian's brain. The moon was full and so bright you could read a paper by it. Such a beautiful sight for such a terrible night of death and destruction. I can never see a full moon without remembering.

The sirens went at about 7 p.m. and we went down the shelter, expecting the usual three or four hours. It was soon obvious that this was going to be more.

The planes came over wave after wave and we could hear the whistle of falling bombs and the noise that incendiary baskets made as they spun around flying the bombs in all directions, the deafening noise of explosion and the smell of the explosive.

Several times we felt the shelter shake, a tremor like I imagine a mild earthquake to be like. Once the blast came through the shelter entrance, bending us over like saplings in a gale. We lost all notion of time and still the moon shone on the town.

The wardens came round to see if we could take in some of the neighbours from the opposite side of the street. Six houses were down and the shelter that side had got flooded. Two children of the Matthews family shared our shelter. Clive, he'd be about eight and his sister Myrtle would be ten.

I don't know how long it was we sat holding their hands, trying to reassure them. They were very quiet.

Again the wardens came round to tell us that we had to evacuate the area as an unexploded land mine had fallen across the main road, top of our street. It was reputed that a land mine could blow up a square mile and later, seeing the devastation caused by a land mine in the Eagle Street area, I think we're lucky to be alive. I was told later that the Home Guard had spotted this object floating down by parachute and at first thought that we were being invaded and shot at it. Lucky they missed. Then when it did come down to earth (it was a coffin-shaped metal canister thing), they thought the Germans were dropping supplies for their invading troops and pulled and dragged it to one side before someone recognised it.

We were all told to leave the shelters and to find somewhere else and to leave the bottom of our street. As we went, people were talking of what had happened. A lady in the next street had been killed and Betty Owen injured. Fred Kilburn also dead fighting the fires in town. The water mains were hit and they were having to let the fires burn.

We all got into the street, there must have been about one hundred people. I'll never forget how it looked. The six houses a pile of rubble, doors off, windows out, roofs off, lamp-post leaning at an angle, when suddenly we heard the whistle of a bomb heading our way. We threw ourselves down on the rubble, a deafening explosion took place and whoosh! Up shot flames higher than the houses, where it had damaged the gas main.

Someone was shouting, 'Get out of here quickly. You're a sitting target.' So we all started to run away, well at least we tried, but had to climb over rubble and watch out for telephone wires and the cables of the tram system which were all down on the floor.

We reached Alfred Herbert's gates and the ARP there said the shelters were full to overflowing and to try the Foleshill Road one. Clambering over rubble we eventually reached it. All the time planes were still passing overhead and bombs were being dropped, but none as close as the one in our street, though.

In the road just outside the shelter was a small bomb crater with an ambulance tipped into it by the front wheels. We crowded into the shelter and people in there asked us where we were from and what was happening? They told us that the police had popped in earlier and told them that the cathedral and all our city centre was bombed, burned and flattened. Other people kept coming in from other areas as they were being evacuated for various reasons. Eventually it began to quieten down and after some time someone went outside to see what was happening. He came back to say that it was getting daylight and he thought the raid was over. No all clear sounded since the sirens had all been damaged.

We crept out of the shelter to find a pall of smoke hanging over everywhere, the smell of burning and dust in the air. We slowly made our way back to our own area, climbing over debris and seeing houses that had been bombed or burnt since our flight past them in the night. Worn out, dejected and numb, we didn't know what to do, but like wounded animals instinctively crept back to our lair.

A warden was still on guard. No, we couldn't go back, it was too dangerous. He didn't know where the rest of the Matthews family was. Not knowing what to do, my dad said he'd walk to work and meet me at the corner of the street again at six and if we couldn't get into the house we could sleep in the shelter at Foleshill again.

It sounds ridiculous looking back, but he was going to walk six miles to the Standard Shadow factory after the experience we'd had, but my dad had been out of work for years during the slump of the '30s. A skilled engineer, he couldn't even get a job sweeping up. So the idea of staying away from work never entered his mind.

He was also a very patriotic man and was on war work and felt he'd be letting our lads down. That winter broke his health and he suffered with his chest for the rest of his days.

We heard that the King had come to see us and had climbed over the rubble and visited people. We were told not to go into town if possible as the dangerous buildings were being blown up by sappers. We heard that Betty Owen had been found in a hospital in Stratford-on-Avon. As she had no identification on her and was too ill to talk, she was a missing person for nearly three weeks.

Our dead were buried in a mass grave and even during the interment we had an air-raid warning.

Soldiers and gangs of men cleared the roads and did emergency repairs to the houses. At night it was like a ghost town with empty trees and tarpaulin flapping in the breeze. Very eerie. Gradually we returned to a semblance of normality.

Sid Lowe was one of a group of soldiers who found themselves stationed in Coventry during the dreadful raid on that city. The scene he witnessed would stay with him for the rest of his life:

My rank was Gunner, Signaller, Royal Artillery. Bit of a novelty, I suppose, with my breeches and puttees, crossed flags, gun-layer's badge. I soon made acquaintance with a group of five or six young chaps, all Coventry lads, some not yet fully kitted out in uniform.

Dark night really upon us now, twenty to seven, here we go again, but what's happening? The clatter of incendiaries and fires starting up all over the place. Within minutes, the whole sky is lit up. We don't need nightfighters here. How easy simply to shoot those bombers right out of the sky, sitting targets. Yet there they were, waiting their turn to unload. I had taken up my position on the number one seat, high up in the latest Mark IX sound locator V1E. Two others, Bill Andrews and Jock Brian, just below. Our equipment was out of order — the previous day a brigadier, along with other officers, had asked if he could try it. Remote control to the guns. Lift the bow slowly and the guns followed it in unison. I never did see how successful it was because he lifted it up quickly and put us out of action.

We shared a tent not far from the cathedral. Our sleeping quarters were only two hundred yards away, wooden huts, yet canvas was as safe as wood, in any case we had to stay beside our equipment simply because there was no safe place of which we knew.

I admired young Jock Brian. He showed no sign of fear as we calmly decided to write a note of farewell to our loved ones. It seems rather melodramatic now to look back and see two soldiers turning an envelope inside out to write a few words to our loved ones. No persons about so I decide on a little walk, to see if I can find something to do to occupy my mind. Maybe a little bomb-happy, but then something most terrible was happening. Another kind of hell. Through the haze and the heat came several horses at full gallop, screaming dogs too, trying to scramble on the backs of the horses.

They passed me by on either side as I stood rooted to the ground. Flames flickered on the horses' manes, tails on fire. One dog wholly on fire screaming in my ear as it brushed my shoulder trying to leap on to a horse.

How long I stood there I do not know. I felt I just could not move. I had heard a horse scream as a little boy, having gone mad and having to be shot, but this was pure hell, another world and looking up to see the cathedral something didn't make sense.

Must be near daybreak when I meet up with a group of five or six, all Coventry lads, when the bombing ceases and through the haze the cathedral looms and a subdued cheer goes up. It had survived.

Twelve hours, I reckoned, and now it was all over. Guess the locals in our battery were already on the way to their homes or to seek out their families.

But it isn't over. A new sound of planes coming in fast, a few seconds, sticks of bombs and as I looked up I saw a different cathedral. Two or three minutes later I found myself inside the shell, with smoke issuing through the masonry.

Joy Bradbury (now Gardner)'s father was a Coventry policeman whose night off coincided with the bombing of the city on 14th November:

My father decided that our Anderson shelter was not really safe, but our next door neighbours had a cellar which was arched (originally a wine cellar). Therefore every night we used to sleep in Jones' cellar.

I was eleven and my sister Gillian was two and a half. My mother had taken the wheels off her pram and she used to sleep in that. My mother and I used to sit upright all night because there was literally nowhere to lie down.

On that particular night the sirens sounded at 7 p.m. The bombing started, horrific, eleven people being killed in a shelter (home-made) two doors from us. My father and my friend's father who lived opposite helped to carry out the bodies.

The all clear went at eleven. We just came up to the living room and waited. Suddenly the windows all came in and there was a mad scramble to the cellar door, which incidentally led off from the living room. Then the sirens went again. We had only one small anti-aircraft situated in Four Pounds Avenue, but that soon became red hot and went out of use.

Mr Jones spent the night in the shelter timing the bombs, whilst my father and Mr Turner toured the streets seeing what could be done. 7 a.m. the all clear sounded. Our house had the back blown in, our old apple trees were all covered with bits and pieces, but I didn't realise they were bits of people from the home-made shelter.

At about 9 a.m. a soldier came to borrow my mother's clothes line to cut off the street because of unexploded bombs. A land mine was dangling between two entries and my father and Mr Turner got the old man out of the house — he had slept through the lot!

In the event my mother put Gillian in a basket which was on the front of her bike and I rode my 'fairy cycle' through all the centre of Coventry — my father guided us through until we got to Foleshill Road where he had to leave us to return to the police station.

We eventually arrived at my aunt's house in Nuneaton at 7 p.m. that evening to be greeted with, 'When are you starting school, Joy?' (My uncle was a teacher, later headmaster.) My aunt said, 'Oh, Alice, we watched it — the sky was brilliant red and do you know, the hatch in the kitchen moved half an inch!'

Elsie Willett recalls living in the centre of the town:

We had a club and were in the cellars when we realised it was getting heavy. The last we saw of the outside was Barton's opposite us and the bullets were flying everywhere. Then I saw Owen Owen go up. Then the horses at the back of us was screaming. Then my neighbours had a torpedo and we lost them all.

When I got outside at 6 a.m. next day the fireman was astounded. They didn't know anyone was so near. One fireman fainted.

Jean Whatley remembers she was fourteen when Coventry was bombed. She was washing her hair when the sirens sounded. Her mother gathered up her personal papers, placed them in her handbag and with her daughter hurried to the nearest air-raid shelter at the local school.

When we got to the shelter there were crowds of people there. We sat on wooden benches all night until seven o'clock the next morning.

When we got home most of the roof and a door were missing from the house. There was no gas or electricity and our pet dog, Rover, had fled.

I went out searching for the dog. Many of the streets were sealed off where time bombs were.

As I walked the streets looking for the dog, an emergency jeep stopped and soldiers gave me a lift halfway home. The dog eventually came home by himself.

When the sirens sounded Jean Long thought it was just another nuisance raid:

I lived next to the canal and several small factories. My husband was abroad in the Royal Artillery. I had a small daughter. I was a postwoman and did first aid. That Thursday evening we had what we called 'a bomber's moon'. We thought it was just another nuisance raid although Lord Haw Haw (the German propaganda broadcaster) said we would have a big raid by ten o'clock. When we realised it was a big raid we went into a neighbour's Anderson shelter.

The bombs were raining down. We heard children screaming, then they stopped. We heard afterwards that five children had been killed in a shelter.

The hours dragged on as we waited for the inevitable bomb. The throb of the German planes, the bells of the fire engines. The ARP wardens came round for the first two or three hours to check. We were too frightened to even move. Four adults, one baby, one dog. We all huddled together waiting for death. The sky was lit up by hundreds of fires, falling masonry, houses on fire, people screaming. For ten hours it was a nightmare. We prayed for the morning to come.

Around 5 a.m. it all went quiet. We waited for the all clear siren. It never came. We didn't dare go out. At about seven we plucked up courage. The sky was blood red. No birds were singing. It was an uncanny silence. Fires were still raging where there was no water, no electricity, no ambulances. Gas mains were fractured, smoke was thick.

One by one people came out, 'if you were one of the lucky

ones'. We went across the road, picking our way through the rubble.

Our house looked all right. My mother pushed the front door and it fell off, and we looked straight through to the bottom of the garden. A bomb had blown out the back of our house. The factory at the back was on fire.

We searched for belongings. All we found was the radio. It wasn't even scratched. Everywhere was devastation. People were quiet. There was no panic, just weary, drawn, pale faces with red-rimmed eyes. Clothes were soiled, some torn, yet in all that I never heard one word of condemnation. Everyone tried to help one another. The bond of friendship and care was very strong.

Margaret Swaley was a qualified physiotherapist who had moved to Coventry to take a job:

I lived in the YWCA and spent many nights in the air-raid shelter, where I passed the time knitting. On 16th November several of us were invited to another YWCA hostel, also in Coventry, so we spent the evening and eventually the night there.

After several hours of much bombing, one of our party had to spend a penny and was told there was toilet just outside the shelter. We were a little surprised to hear a tinkle, tinkle but were more surprised when someone who didn't know what it was cried out in alarm, 'It's the church bells! The German paratroops have landed.'

Irene Dore recalls her time as a student nurse in a large training hospital when the war started. She left training school in 1940 and joined a Cardiff nursing agency. From there she was transferred to Coventry and hardly had time to settle in her new surroundings when she found herself on night duty in the hospital's scarlet fever ward:

All were children with the exception of a pregnant mum. All patients had settled down for the night, and what a lovely calm evening it was — despite the black-out there was a bright, full moon. Suddenly all hell broke loose. The air-raid sirens shattered our ears and almost immediately the bomber planes were overhead.

The memory is so vivid I can see it clearly — so clearly — even now. In an adjoining field was an air force ack-ack unit with many balloons flying above. The bombs were now raining down. Carrying the tiny tots — some clinging to our white aprons — we made for the air-raid shelters. A few yards from the ward entrance was a vast steaming crater — a land mine, and part of the ward had collapsed.

Running back to the ward, I could see some RAF men trying to control blazing balloons. Fires were raging all around. It was as if the lights had been switched on — you could have read a newspaper.

Patients were trapped in the ward debris; several RAF men and medical staff were raising a heavy beam off the pregnant patient. An injection of morphine was called for. Another whistling bomb was heard coming for us, a spontaneous 'cluck' came from one of the men and the beam came down with a thud.

By now it was so light — not only bombs were still dropping, but planes were flying low and using machine-guns. There was no returning gunfire from the ack-ack guns. They had quickly run out of ammunition.

I really cannot remember the following day. I do remember the following night. What little food we had was served on unwashed crockery. Baths that were still remaining held the only water we had. Remaining patients slept on mattresses on the floor. I sat on the floor between, holding the hands of the children on each side.

For those in hospital as patients, the air-raid siren was even more terrifying. Many were unable to move and relied completely on the nursing staff. Others, like Dennis Hill, were casualties of the bombing who found themselves being rushed to hospital for emergency treatment:

We lived in Coventry at the time of the November blitz. To be out on this night was exciting for a thirteen-year-old boy because the reason was to collect shrapnel from the bombs — incendiaries that sometimes failed to go off — and from the anti-aircraft shells. The biggest prize of all was the cap from an anti-aircraft shell.

They had a brass timing-device inside that was very fascinating to a young boy. My friends and I all had our own collections, thus I was outside on this night, which was unique in that the bombing started early on in the evening and of course, which we did not know then, was going to be the heaviest air-raid in England since the start of the war.

It was a cold crisp moonlit night — like bonfire night. We became aware early in the evening that it was going to be a heavier raid than usual and I could hear voices in the darkness saying, 'We are in for it tonight!' Suddenly the whole street was lit up by incendiaries. I had been standing by the front door — my mother, sister and two children sheltering underneath the stairs. My brother-in-law was an air-raid warden and my father was out in the back garden.

I ran into the street, picked up a sand-bag and threw it over an incendiary bomb which was lying in the gutter. That very second it exploded and I was thrown backwards and then realized that I could not see. Footsteps came running and someone said, 'We must get him to hospital!' Then another voice said, 'I will get my car out and take him' — there were few people who owned cars in those days.

The hospitals, fire engines and ambulances were all in the city centre, so we made our way into the city. To me it sounded like an enormous bonfire night. Bombs coming down made one kind of noise and anti-aircraft guns another sound. As we tried to make our way to Coventry and Warwickshire Hospital (which was bombed that night) a policeman stopped the car and said, 'You will never get through, all the roads are blocked. Your best plan is to go to Gulson Hospital.' This was situated a short distance from the city centre.

After many diversions we eventually arrived at the hospital. The raid by this time was at its height. All I could hear was clamour, crying and sobbing. I was handed over to a nurse and someone said, 'This boy is blind.' I can remember thinking that I will be blind forever and also I won't be able to collect all the shrapnel that will be lying around in the morning.

I was put into a bed and the first thing I heard was, 'The ward is on fire!' In the morning the ward was evacuated. I think it was a converted bus that took us to an emergency hospital in Rugby. My eyes had been sealed together by the blast and my eyebrows and the front of my hair singed off.

It was a week before my parents were able to find out where I was, as everywhere was chaos. When they came to see me I can remember my elderly father being annoyed that he had lost his best overcoat which had been thrown over me and my mother concerned over the ordeal of having to cook over the fire because there was no gas.

I was in hospital for two weeks and people would stop by the bed and say, 'This little boy is blind' and I would lie there feeling quite heroic. I can remember falling in love with the voice of the ward sister who was very kind to me. For quite some time I would cycle over to Rugby and see her.

When I returned to school I was asked where I had been, and when I said in hospital no-one seemed very interested.

I found out later that one of my classmates had been killed that night.

Ron Patten and his friend Den Burdett were accustomed to the occasional raid on Coventry and were not concerned when once again the warning sirens began:

At this time my friend and I were regularly out in the streets, putting out incendiary bombs either in houses or simply in the streets. We both became adept at dismantling the charges from the incendiary bombs which had failed to explode — God knows what would have happened had any of these bombs been booby-trapped.

We rarely used the shelters, preferring to be in the thick of things, but on one occasion we had found a 'dud' incendiary bomb and after dismantling it we decided we wouldn't keep it as a souvenir as we had enough. We thought that we would hand it in to the chief air-raid warden at the nearby shelters.

Although it was perfectly safe in its unassembled state, we little knew how much trouble this would cause. As soon as we entered the shelter carrying the defused incendiary bomb the women started screaming, 'A bomb! A bomb! Get it out of here!' I had never encountered such hysteria. When we tried to explain that it was safe the warden told us to put it in a bucket of water and take the bucket outside.

Amid shouts of abuse, and hysteria, Den and I quickly retired outside (with the bucket).

We decided that we would never again enter an air-raid shelter.

Thomas Parry was nine. His father was a senior air-raid warden who was off duty when the siren sounded:

At approximately 9.30 p.m. all hell broke loose. The house next door received a direct hit. The lights went out and brick and rubble were everywhere. The door which led under the stairs split into four pieces and was jammed solid by the weight of the masonry against it. All was silent, then we heard muffled voices. 'Are you all right?' Dad and his colleagues began digging away and after what seemed like hours a torch-light appeared and frantic movement to release all of us trapped.

After about three-quarters of an hour we all managed to crawl through a hole into the front room that was. A man whose name I never knew said, 'I will take this lad to my house.' At which time he picked me up and away we went.

Having got about a hundred yards, a bomb came down, a direct hit, on his house. He did no more than leave me lying on the pavement and went to see how best he could save his family. By this time my mum and dad were with me.

My dad said, 'Let's get out into the country.' So without further ado we started walking to what was considered a safe area (the fields on the outskirts of the city). We had gone about half a mile when we were dive-bombed. Dad then insisted we take shelter. The nearest building was the Co-Op bakery and the three of us went in under the tables.

The rats there were so numerous that we found them running over our feet. Dad then decided that the place was unsafe and we should move on. We did, but due to the intensity of the bombing it took us half an hour to crawl 500 yards to the public house in which we sheltered for the remainder of the raid.

About 6.30 a.m. the all clear sounded and the three of us went outside to witness unbelievable sights. Tram-lines standing up like soldiers, houses and shops demolished, roads blocked. An unexploded bomb on the corner of the street where we lived. Our own house partially collapsed, roof gone and a piece of tram-line embedded in the bathroom that was.

At that moment in time Dad made a decision. We would all try and go to a friend's house in the neighbouring town of Nuneaton. So we started walking.

It's eleven miles and we walked all the way. They were only too pleased to see us unscathed.

Brenda Mendenhall remembers going to the cinema with her father. The film was Hurricane:

We could hear the guns above the film and when it was over we left to make our way home. We ran to a side street to one of the brick shelters outside a laundry. We stayed there for about half an hour and an old lady joined us. She was crying and clinging to me. I was sixteen at the time. Then a couple came in who knew the lady and they took her home.

Dad and I left the shelter and ran again up the road. The laundry and the shelter were hit just as we left. Luckily no one else was in there. We ran to the common. There was a large underground shelter there so we went into that, and stayed there for some hours. Bombs were dropped on the common and even in the shelter we got terrific blasts from them which made many people scream and run further along the shelter.

Dad and I just sat. I think we had had enough. We arrived home at 7 a.m. to find we only had the kitchen window broken, but no water, gas or electricity. I just got ready and went to work as usual.

Kenneth Farrell was 22 when an incendiary bomb destroyed his family's two bedrooms:

The fire was put out by the vicar of Holy Trinity Church before the brigade arrived. A sealed off gas-pipe was unsealed by the

126

heat and lit up. Mother was rather uncomplimentary to an ARP warden who called, 'Put that light out!'

Time and again there were reports of the 'ordinary people' doing remarkable things. Jean Rees recalls that Coventry under siege was no exception:

My father was a hero of the bombings. He was one of two men who worked at the emergency mortuary in Hill Street and had to piece together bodies of all the unfortunate people who were killed and box them up. He used to raise his hat to them each night when he left.

Barbara Smith lived with her family in Birmingham. Her father was a policeman and had been sent with a special force to Coventry to give what assistance he could:

I well remember his return. He looked pale and haggard — told us that he had not slept, eaten or even rested for three days; and when my mother said quietly, 'What was it like, dear?', he answered, 'Terrible' and burst into tears. At the age of thirteen I had never seen a man cry.

The full horror of the Coventry blitz and its effects were described in a letter written to Norman Bedford's mother by her sister just ten days after the raid:

My dear Alice,

Many, many thanks for your letter. I wonder if you received Len's postcard, for on the Friday following the raid, him and Cis went to Northampton till Sunday and he sent you a card to let you know that we were safe.

Alice, I shall never forget it as long as I live. My nerve has completely gone, I dread the dark and the siren. The planes came over every minute, and they started on Green Lane at 7.45 p.m. I was sitting by the fire reading the paper, when the roar of the guns and bombs was deafening, and George, Dad and I went to the back door to look. There was hundreds of flares dropped and tracer bullets going up, and the moon was brilliant. Dad couldn't understand why they dropped flares, for the night was like day. Suddenly we saw the roof on the corner house collapse and we all drew back by the kitchen table and we held each other in grim death as the front door of the house blew in and at the same time light, gas and water went off. We are still without it.

A mine had dropped in Beanfield Avenue, killed half way down that street. The bus came to carry away the dead and when it turned the corner into Beanfield a bomb came down and over it went. We had a bit of a fire in the grate and that blew out. George and Dad picked it up and threw it back, else we should have had the house on fire.

We all stood crouched in the hall, you know, between the two doors, sick with fright and at eleven o'clock they dropped a mine on the corner of Harold's row and poor Harold has lost all. They only just got out in time. The blast from there blew our back in, and God, the way we clung together we thought our end had come. The roof fell over and the fall of the plaster, we really thought the house was falling on us.

There wasn't a minute's break for a solid eleven hours and later on the guns gave out for want of ammunition, so of course, the buggers had it all to themselves.

You wouldn't know Coventry. The whole town is down, nothing but mass rubble. All those beautiful shops, Boots, Flinns, the jewellers all along there, down Smithford Street, Marks, Woolworths, gone, not a shop standing anyway. Well, 500 planes, one a minute. All factories are down, George's place is gutted and even after over a week, the place is burning in parts.

My darling, it was a nightmare. I pray to God that you never experience it.

Prior to this terrible slaughtering of Coventry I had not been out of this house for three solid months, so you can imagine the effect it took.

At 6.30 the next morning the all clear went and I was as you have always seen me, in slacks and that jumper you made me. It has been a Godsend to me and it is as black as hell. You wouldn't think it was pink, and I had on Dad's greatcoat. I waddled along to Harold to see if he was all right. God the sight that met my eyes. I'll never forget it. Nothing but charred ruins and I thought they must be under it. I shed buckets of tears — and since — but they had just got out. As the mine dropped by them they ran under fire to a shelter in Woodside. Poor Harold has lost all, I can't help but think of that.

Friday night it rained like hell, to add irony to our fate, but luckily in the morning we got all the beds downstairs and pushed them all down here. We have no bedrooms to sleep in, the roofs are gone but George scratched his head on Saturday morning and said, 'Charlie, we will have to do something to the roof' and he was wondering where to get a ladder when a bright idea struck him. Get through the loft and work that way and they did, placing the tiles in position and, without a word, pinching them from the next roof.

I wouldn't mind if we could get the wireless and were able to look out the boarded-up windows. I feel just like a prisoner and it is such a job cooking on this little fire. My poor back, but I mustn't grumble, I and ours have our lives and up to the present I have my reason. Alice, I think sometimes I shall go mad.

When dawn broke on the Friday morning and we saw the damage, glass and plaster everywhere, our poor ceiling papers that Horace had put on, stairs all thick with plaster, honestly, we didn't know where to start. But Dad was a brick. He got into it right away and that night he had broken up for four days' holiday.

It was a good job he was at home. I don't know what I should have done without him. George is still on salvage work and when that is finished, God knows what will happen. Their place is down and they still have 400 tons of coal burning. They can't get it out.

I do sincerely hope Norman enjoyed his part, bless him, we may have the luck to see him now, else that night we didn't think we'd see anyone again, but please God we are here for a little while longer. Must close now, my head hurts and these ruddy candles get on my nerves.

Len is working. They had the roof off but the machinery isn't damaged. There are two or three firms at work now.

I am so tired, all my love to you and a big hug and kiss for Norman, and give my love to Horace, I hope he doesn't have to leave you.

Ever yours,
Jonah

xxxxxxx

PS: Had a letter from Dorothy and like you have offered me their place and her mum wants me to go there, but you know what I am, I must be here to welcome George, Dad and Len with a fire and a hot meal. Alice, I couldn't leave them to come home to a desolate place. You wouldn't. Ah well, let's hope for better times. My only hope is the buggers don't visit us again for a while, anyway. Last night was the first night since the blitz we had no warning.

Love, it was grand and up to now the siren hasn't gone and it is close to nine o'clock, touch wood, but they have been over in the day as well. We did shoot one down yesterday in Stoneleigh Abbey.

Once more good night, my darling. xxxxx

Although Jonah decided to stay in Coventry, many felt the need to leave the city and seek out the safety of the countryside. Shirley Goode was six years old and moved with her parents each night to a small village outside of Coventry. Her father's job gave him an allowance for extra petrol, making it possible for the family to be mobile.

Mum and Dad found someone to let us have a room over a shop in a nearby village, so each evening we drove to the village to sleep away from the raids and return the next morning.

The day after the bombing of the cathedral my dad drove Mum and me to see the ruins and as we came back via Hershall Common, we saw thousands of people clutching a few possessions and all walking away from town.

8

The Blitz Spreads

Had the Germans followed up the raid on Coventry with more of the same, British industry would have suffered a devastating setback. Yet within weeks of the one heavy attack, most of the factories of Coventry were once again working at full production.

Goering, apparently satisfied that Coventry had been dealt a fatal blow, remained convinced that the plan to incapacitate the industrial areas of Britain was a good one. He decided to concentrate on other Midlands cities, especially Birmingham, and also to attack Southampton.

Living in Southampton, Emily Dimmock had seen plenty of action. Much of the Battle of Britain had been fought overhead; she had waved to paddle-steamers off shore as they made their way across the Channel to pick up the remains of Britain's army fleeing from Dunkirk; and seen barrage balloons by the dozens find their way to earth with the help of raiding Luftwaffe pilots. But the Germans were not going to stop her wedding:

The morning of my wedding day brought an air-raid warning before breakfast, so it was eat breakfast in the shelter, the all clear went and we went indoors to erect the wedding cake. There was more gunfire, so we took it down again and it accompanied us to the shelter, where we left it for safety until we came back from the church.

We were due at the church at 10 a.m. and my brother was to give me away. He had spent the night working at an aircraft factory at Hamble where he was an aircraft inspector and the air-raid alerts meant he had to take shelter and the time of his journey home was trebled.

There was no time for nerves, pre-wedding or otherwise, because everyone had gone to church and I was the only one left to run around and help him get ready.

We did get to the church on time, but air-raid warnings interrupted the service and we had to go to the crypt. No photographs — no photographer or photographic materials available for such trimmings to a wedding. No honeymoon either, although one had been arranged, but had we gone out of Southampton at that time we would not have been allowed back in. No-one came into Southampton then without being a person vital to the war effort.

Wedding guests from Winchester travelling by bus were held up by soldiers boarding the bus. We brought strong walking shoes as it was freely rumoured that the civilian population of Southampton would be evacuated and we'd have to walk, but Hitler's barges of troops on the other side of the Channel were bombed by the RAF and he decided not to invade by sea.

I can still remember the eerie feeling when we went out of our back door when the night raids were so heavy and we were confronted with a night sky lit up like daylight with Very lights hanging like candelabra over us and the incendiary bombs everywhere, the smell of burning and the crackling sounds. We were armed with garden spades and forks, plus the coal shovel and anything else we could find, and set about piling earth from the garden on the fire bombs and patting some out with the tools, but we were driven into the shelter when bombers came in over the flares and dropped high explosives.

We were joined by unknown people who just came into our shelter shocked and dumb and went out again when the all clear sounded without our ever knowing who they were.

Doris Hayman (now Bird) was seventeen and living in Sale, near Manchester, at the time of the blitz:

It was impossible to sleep or feel safe even in the Anderson shelter below ground, so most of us muffled up against the cold and stayed outside. My father, Joe Hayman (a veteran of the First World War), and I stood on the cobbled stones in Britannia Road and watched in horror as Sale Town Hall burned.

The clock, the beautiful dance floor and the whole top floor disintegrated. I was absolutely terrified and trembling. I clutched my new black court shoes to my bosom and decided that if I was going to heaven then my shoes were going with me.

The day Patricia Sample arrived home from evacuation, she went to visit a friend of her father's who had a pub in Manchester:

The sirens went about 7 to 7.30 p.m. We didn't take much notice at first and then the bombing became really heavy. We all went down to the underground canal that runs beneath Deansgate. It was full of beds as far as I could see. The men, including my father, were asked to volunteer, putting out fires from incendiary bombs. My mother and I thought we would never see him again. The noise and the thuds were terrifying — women were fainting. The Red Cross were working non-stop and we were told that the whole of Deansgate above us was on fire and Victoria Station had gone. Most of the exits were blocked and people were trying not to panic, but many were suffering from claustrophobia and rushing from exit to exit only to find them blocked by falling buildings.

Eventually, to my joy, we caught sight of my father. He came down the original exit which was still unblocked. He was exhausted after four hours of fire-fighting. I remember my mother saying that they were trying to extinguish incendiary bombs on the flat roofs of buildings but were greatly hampered by guard dogs on many of the properties.

We surfaced to the most devastating sight I have ever seen. We were worried about my grandma and eventually found our car. It was still there. Not a window left and covered in white ash with a half-burned-out incendiary bomb on the roof. We got in and it actually started. We drove to All Saints. The beautiful church had gone, but thank heavens we found our gran crying outside the shop. My gran was so happy to see that we were all alive.

Tom Dunne was eleven and living in Manchester with his parents. His father had refused a shelter, believing that the Germans would never be able to bomb the area where they lived. One particularly heavy raid occurred in December:

In the house were my older brother Eddie, aged thirteen, my younger brother Paul, aged six and Leo, the baby, aged eighteen months, who was asleep in his cot in the back bedroom. I remember a neighbour calling and begging my dad to share his air-raid shelter — Dad refused. Later Paul and I went to bed, in the same room as Leo but sleeping in a double bed. The blitz continued, but like most children we soon fell asleep. My next memory was waking up and I was floating upwards, it seemed in slow motion. The roof was opening up and I was flying towards the stars. No pain, no special sensation – the oblivion. A parachute mine had done its job.

How long I was unconscious is open to conjecture, but it must have been several hours, for reasons which I will explain later. When I woke up I was choking with brick dust, cold and very dazed; I was buried in my bed. Clearing my nose, mouth and eyes, I could see that the roof had gone and that there was no rear wall to the house or dividing walls. Looking to my right I could see that Leo's cot was no longer there, just a pile of rubble. One thing that really imprinted itself in my mind was that standing upright in a corner section of the bedroom wall was a large statue of 'Our Lady'.

I realised that I must get myself up to dig for Leo and was clearing debris off myself, when Paul, who up to this point I had not thought about, started moving under rubble near me. I was free and started digging. Luckily he was not buried deeply and seemed unhurt. When I uncovered him he became hysterical and I virtually remember slapping his face to stop him — which he did. He lay quietly and I told him I must try and find baby Leo. I started digging with bare hands near to the corner, lifting rubble and placing it in the region of my bed. I kept finding pieces of the cot, no bigger than a cigarette package, and I really felt I was not going to find my baby brother. Suddenly I heard a whimper. I speeded up the digging and there he was. All his night clothes were missing and he was naked and jet black. I cleared his mouth and eyes and lifted him up into my arms — apparently none the worse. He cried loudly — it was a wonderful sound. Then and only then did I think of shouting for help, which I did very loudly — Paul joined in.

Our shouts really startled the rescuers outside in Platt Lane, who were just keeping a watching brief on the devastation, waiting for daylight to dig our bodies out. We had apparently been unconscious for so long that the emergency/rescue services had removed my mother's body from the downstairs living room (she was killed instantly), removed my brother Eddie (who was slightly injured) and my father, who was only dazed. Unfortunately my father had wandered off in his shocked state and sustained major head injuries (not fatal) from anti-aircraft shrapnel which was falling like rain. They had searched for us and had obviously concluded that we were dead.

At the police station, we were made comfortable with blankets and cocoa. Outside, the blitz raged on unabated. I was still dazed. Suddenly a bomb landed near the police station, at the back and shook the building. Some time later a policeman came in screaming that his wife and children had just been killed. A police sergeant tried to pacify him and nodded towards us lying there and said, 'Calm down. You are not the only one with trouble.'

Sheila Wright was seven. She had been evacuated to Boscombe in Devon, but by November, 1940 was back with her parents in Southampton when the siren went once more:

I was running down the garden path. I looked up at the sky. It was bright stars and the beams from the searchlights were criss-crossing the sky. Then the guns began firing again and the noise was as bad as ever. I reached the opening to the shelter. I wanted to jump down into its safety, but I just couldn't move. My mother was behind me, telling me to get in and then shouting at me. I could hear her, but still stood there frozen to the spot. My dad pushed my mother out of the way, picked me up and threw me into the shelter. Once I was inside I began to cry and shake.

My parents comforted me and my father explained that although I didn't think I was afraid, I really had been too terrified to move.

Lorna Jones remembers working in a solicitor's office in her home town of Southampton:

As the raids worsened we were sent to the public shelter under Holy Rood Church, where we had to waste many hours until the all clear sounded. My mother and I were coming back from lunch when without any warning we saw a formation of enemy planes approaching. We dived for the back door, hoping to make it to the Anderson shelter, but outside the sunny day had turned to night by the bombs already falling and the debris thrown up.

Bryan Savage's father, a veteran of the First World War, spent three nights a week fire-watching at his office in the centre of Birmingham and the remaining nights at home:

He was a man with life strictly timetabled and each night when at home he would have his supper in the living room and listen to the midnight news on the radio whilst eating, despite the air-raids.

Exactly on the stroke of Big Ben's midnight chime, the whole house shook following a tremendous explosion. My brother, sister and I rushed up the steps of the cellar to the ground floor, through the bricks, broken furniture and choking dust into the living room. There we found Dad unconscious with his face in the supper dish, festooned in the washing that had been on the clothes airer which used to be fastened to the ceiling and was moved up and down by a rope pulley.

The bomb had exploded just behind the houses on the other side of the road and the substantial blast had brought down our substantial chimney. My father had caught the full force of the cast-iron frame of the thing and was knocked out.

Marion Sutton was just fifteen. She was living in Birmingham and remembers seeing her first German aircraft:

I ran to the window as it came over and saw the explosions of the three bombs. These were only small bombs, but of course everyone was horrified and flocked in their hundreds the next day to see the damage. One house was split into two and the husband and wife landed one in the front and one in the back garden. The St John's Ambulance ran the ambulances that day and a friend on duty that night told me of her horror in finding that the man had a leg missing. She was greatly relieved when he said, 'Don't worry, lady, I always leave it in the corner of the room when I go to bed.'

R. W. Wright had taken shelter in the cellar of his Birmingham butcher's shop. It had a tiled floor, a tap, drain and, most important, three exits:

I was by myself and frightened to death, of course, but hungry, so I was busy cooking a lamb chop, which I had dangling on a bit of wire in front of an electric fire with a tin on the floor to catch the fat. A loaf of bread and a bottle of beer and oh, a bottle of tomato sauce.

It was about 8 p.m. I hadn't quite got to my chop, when our bomb fell. It fell through Marshall's roof, straight through four storeys and down into Marshall's cellar where it hit the wall at a tangent, which deflected it slightly sideways into the floor about twelve feet and around fifteen feet sideways. It actually came to rest underneath where I was sitting.

The cellar shook like a boat. The lights went out and so did I, pretty quickly, I can tell you. Well, I found an air-raid warden who found the police who found the AFS who found the bomb disposal squad. All these people, one after the other, I guided down Marshall's cellar to view the mess and the hole down which the bomb had disappeared. The conclusion? A delayed-action bomb, so everyone was kicked out who lived anywhere near. A rope was stretched across Bryton Road and Edward Road and no-one could go into this forbidden area.

All that night the bombs kept falling. I spent most of the time hiding behind the sand-bags which were filled up in front of the library.

When morning came I was tired out, as you can imagine, and in despair wondered what the hell to do. There was the shop, full of meat and no-one allowed to go near. By this time my staff, Albert Burford, whom we used to call Skylark, his wife Dorothy or Doll and his half-brother John arrived. Well, I remembered that about half a mile down the road was an empty shop which used to sell fish. So I asked if we could get the key, which we soon did.

The neighbours supplied hot water and we soon cleaned up the shop. Then we went back to the road barrier and asked Inspector Swift to allow us to go into our shop and get our supplies.

'Certainly not,' he said. 'The slightest tremor could set off that delayed-action bomb and blow up half the district.'

Well, anyway, we decided to take a chance and went down Clifton Road around the back, climbed over a few walls and we were in. That is Skylark, John and me. Frightened to death, we were. We sneaked about on tip-toe. We didn't even start the van, but pushed it towards the fridge and loaded up with everything like knives, saws and scales and I don't know what else.

Then we carefully opened the yard gates and pushed the van into the road and down to the barricade where Inspector Swift was having a fit.

Well, anyway, he didn't like to tell us to take it back, so we strung a notice on the rope which told anyone who wanted to know that Wright's, the butchers, was now temporarily transferred to Mosely Road where it would be business as usual.

On Tuesday afternoon I suddenly remembered our little dog. We had a small Pekinese bitch named Sandy and she had pups about as big as a duck's egg. So back I went and nipped back to the shop. There was a side door to the living quarters which were behind and over the shop. So I opened the door and gave a nice soft whistle and out trotted Sandy and her two pups.

All the people watching cheered. You'd have thought we'd won the war.

Soon after this the bomb-disposal squad arrived and started digging. I told them where I thought the bomb was, but they wouldn't listen to me and faithfully followed the path the missile had made, making a nice tunnel, properly shored up and everything. It took a long while to reach our bomb, I can tell you. Till morning, in fact. Then the brave soldiers dragged the thing back up until it rested on the floor of the cellar, underneath some iron doors which opened on to the pavement above.

The next thing was to tie a rope around the bomb and trail it up the stairs, over the pavement and across the road where the rest of the squad, about eight or ten of them, were standing.

I can remember them gathering around like a tug-of-war team under the leadership of the sergeant, who stood by and shouted, 'Heave!' which they did, with some success, too. 'Heave!' shouted the sergeant and the bomb moved up another foot or two. All the people watching stood very quiet and fascinated, waiting to see the bomb appear up from the cellar and on to the pavement. 'Heave!' shouted the sergeant and there it was at last. Just peeping over the pavement edge. 'Heave!' shouted the sergeant and they did. Then the rope broke. All the tug-of-war team went arse over tip into a great pile of arms and legs. On the other side of the road our bomb, which would explode at the slightest tremor, fell back down the stairs with a very satisfied 'thud' to the floor again.

Well, all this was too much for the audience who all burst out into spontaneous laughter and applause. The soldiers picked themselves up with sheepish grins, dusted themselves down, tied the rope together into a great big bow and started again. After several good heaves the bomb at last was dragged out. All 500 lbs of it, and rolled down the pavement into the gutter.

The lieutenant then sent all the squad, except the sergeant, away. The barriers were moved another fifty yards up the street — and us, of course. Then believe it or not the sarge sat astride the bomb and attacked it with a hammer and chisel. After a good few bangs he threw the hammer down and let it be known that the thing was harmless.

It wasn't a delayed-action bomb at all. Just the fuse was a dud. The rope barriers were taken away and all the crowd gathered around to congratulate the soldiers and view the bomb. By this time the hat was being passed around and a goodly sum was collected and passed to the lieutenant and his crew.

We hurried into the shop to try and get things ship-shape and start up business again.

Amid all the devastation there was always something that escaped. Beryl Room recalls emerging after a thirteen-hour blitz of Birmingham to find that the whole street had been destroyed:

At the end of the raid we went to look for where our house had been and there among the debris stood our piano with hardly a scratch on it. Also the family cat was sitting on top of it having a wash!

Sonia Waller was allowed to go to the entrance of her shelter near Liverpool and watch the bombers overhead. She does not remember being frightened, only excited:

As a family my mother would play and encourage us to sing around the piano. One day when I must have been about five and just at school, my mother asked me to choose a song — I asked her for the air-raid shelter hymn. She eventually found out that I meant, 'Oh God our help in ages past . . . our "shelter" from the stormy blast.'

Marshall Litherland and his mother arrived home after a raid to find all the windows and the front door had been blown in. They had two new velvet chairs in the front room of their Liverpool home:

As children we were never allowed to sit on them. My mother was buying them through a club at so much per week. The chairs were ruined by soot and broken glass and, ironically, she still had to pay for these for many months after they were destroyed. My mother made an effort to clean up the mess and to gather together some personal belongings. Whilst she was doing this her sister came in very distressed. I overheard her say to my mother, 'Your mother's gone.'

Now my old grandma used to visit the communal shelters during the evenings and it was during this night that she went to the Durning Road College, together with many hundreds more, to shelter from the bombs, deep down in the cellars of the school.

On this particular night the college received a direct hit from a land mine and the building was completely destroyed. Eight people crawled out from beneath the rubble, my grandmother being one of them. We did not know that she had survived until many days later. She evacuated herself on the day after the raid and told no one. We found out a week later when we received a letter through the post.

Sheila McAllister remembers she was six when the bombing started, and had a brother aged eighteen months. Her parents decided that, rather than evacuate their daughter from the Birkenhead area, they would all stick together. They had an Anderson shelter in the garden.

My mother grew nasturtiums on it and tomatoes around the door. Sheltered by a doorway of sand-bags they did very well. We also had interesting wildflowers, courtesy of the load of soil from Wales brought to cover the shelter.

Inside we were very cramped at first and it was impossible for adults to lie down. However, an extra length of corrugated iron was added, which gave about six feet by five. We had bunks on one side for the kids and a well chocked-up old camp-bed for adults to sit on. I don't think they slept much. We had a heavy iron paraffin stove for heat, light and boiling kettles, which it did fairly well. In my siren-suit, made from my father's old serge suit, I was warm, if rather itchy.

We were put to bed there for months. The usual inhabitants were my mother, we two children, the small baby from next door and his mother, who tended to get hysterical when things hotted up. My mother didn't. She had a carving knife for the first German who showed his face!

After one raid we had no windows left anywhere but the kitchen. People over the back from us called out that they had to evacuate for an unexploded bomb. We ended up with fifteen people in that one kitchen and two dogs which hated each other. We had no water, but we had gas. My mother was cooking several minuscule weekend joints, everyone's meat hastily snatched up in the exodus. An exhausted man was asleep against the kitchen door with his tin hat over his eyes. I had never seen an adult so filthy. He, with my father, had been on the streets all night.

Diana Jones (now Palmer) was eleven and part of a large family living in Liverpool. Her parents had a confirmed shelter space under the fish market in the city centre:

We had our mattresses and bedding left down there. It was a horrible place, and my elder sister and I used to go to the Capital Cinema when we could, even though the sirens had started, to delay the moment of going to bed. We would walk through the black-out into town, watching bombs fall and searchlights and the mobile artillery firing at the enemy. Looking back we were either totally stupid or fearless. Anything to delay that horrible shelter.

The stench was fearsome, it was packed with children, mothers, old men. There must have been some way for us to obtain hot water for tea, for we always had a hot drink.

We had grown used to the bombing, shrapnel etc, but this one night stands out in my memory.

The alert had sounded and we were in the fish market. We were all tired, night after night of bombing, sleep was hard to come by, too much talking and air-raid wardens coming and telling everyone of thousands of bombers overhead. Liverpool burning.

Then there was a great uproar. My dad grabbed my next-to-youngest sister who for some reason had huge swollen legs, my mum carried the youngest one and we were being led up many stairs. On the way we had to walk through gas escaping from the refrigerators. The stairs seemed to go on and on and in a circular way. We could smell smoke and burning. Where we came out, I don't know to this day but the air was thick with smoke, everywhere was burning. One of my sisters was sick and dizzy with the gas, we had been sleeping on the wet ground, firemen were black and exhausted.

My dad, my frail old dad, somehow managed to keep carrying my sick sister and keep us together. There was panic. Lots and lots of aeroplanes, the sky red, people running searching for shelter, bombs and fire bombs exploding all over. My mum and dad led us across the road to where the old Forum Cinema was burning. We ran under the ladders of the fire-fighters with flames and smoke and debris all around. Some splinters hit me, everywhere people were running. This way and that searching for shelter.

My dad spotted an open doorway opposite Blacklers, also well ablaze, with two air-raid wardens looking up at the sky. He got us across the road, the warden said that there was no room but my dad begged him to let us in for the children's sake. He said, 'Hurry up, I'll have to close the door, they're packed like sardines down there.'

This shelter was under a butcher's shop, where St John's market now stands. It was so full there was no room to sit. The smell from the overflowing buckets used for WC purposes was something I'll remember always. We all leaned on each other. People were banging on the door upstairs begging to be let in. It was impossible. Many people wandered around searching and died that night.

Towards dawn or thereabouts it had been quiet for a while and my elder sister and I could stand the smell of the place no longer and told my dad we were going home. He let us go.

We came out to a beautiful red sky and smoke and flames, also an unexploded bomb lying at the side of the shelter we were in. Its nose was buried in the concrete and soldiers were around it.

It was an amazing sight. My sister and I just wandered around for a bit, glad to be able to move, looking at all the shops on fire or just burned out and smouldering. There were men digging in the debris, searching for people and dragging out bodies. We reached Lewis's, just a shell now, and made our way home up Brownlow Hill.

We saw lorries piled with dead people being covered with tarpaulin and when the lorries moved the bodies wobbled under the tarpaulin.

We met our brother in his naval uniform, his face and uniform were black, his eyes so tired and hurt-looking. He had been on leave and had left his new-born daughter and wife to help with rescue work. He pushed his cap up and was nearly crying. I heard the helpless anger in his voice when he told how he'd dug half-burned dead women and children out of the ruins. He said at least we, meaning the forces, can fight back.

That was the last time we saw our brother. He sailed a few days later and was reported missing in action.

Louis Day was a fifteen-year-old lad living in Liverpool. He had just been given his first bike and was planning a trip with his friend to nearby Chester. When Liverpool was badly raided on the Saturday, it looked as though his Sunday outing would be postponed:

As the bombs were getting increasingly closer, Mum got us up from bed and we huddled in the corner of the small brick shelter. There was my mum, my sister Sylvia, aged ten, and me. Dad was on fire-watching duty that night and so was outside on the streets keeping a look-out with a companion for incendiary bombs. He popped back every now and again to see that we were all right.

About ten minutes after he had been in to see us on the last occasion, the bombing bangs and thuds got closer and closer until there was the most almighty crash and all the lights went out. Brick dust filled the air but we couldn't see a thing. After a minute or so Mum produced a flash-lamp and we could see that our little shelter was the only thing still standing. The cellar had collapsed, completely obliterating the beds. Broken beams were down to the floor and rubble was everywhere.

Some time later we heard a faint voice calling. We thought it was Dad but it was in fact a police search-party looking for survivors.

We all three shouted, 'Help! Help!' as loud as we could and we were very relieved when our cries were answered. The faint sound of digging could be heard and after a while a small hole was forced through in the vicinity of the grating which was above our heads. A small stirrup-pump hose was fed down to us and I sprayed the water on the fast-approaching flames. About fifteen minutes later, the rescuers made a hole big enough for us to be pulled out of the shelter one at a time. When we got out we were amazed to see that we were on the edge of a tremendous crater which was a mass of flames. We were taken by ambulance to Bootle Hospital and quite miraculously not one of us had a scratch.

We found out shortly afterwards that the crater had been caused by two parachute land mines which had tangled together and our father was caught in the blast and killed instantly.

I returned to the crater a week or two later. It was still smouldering slightly and there at the very bottom was what remained of my new bike. A twisted heap of tubes. I borrowed some tools and removed the three-speed gears for future use. This and my dad's broken pipe was all we salvaged.

Constance Bolton lived near Liverpool and had been in hospital for seven weeks. After two operations in three weeks she could not be moved, even during an air-raid:

All patients were put under the beds while I was piled up with pillows, so the nurse kept popping her head out from under the bed to say, 'Are you all right, love?'

Jean McWilliam was a twelve-year-old schoolgirl living in Wallasey when the Germans turned their attention to Merseyside. Her father was a headmaster and therefore exempt from call-up to the forces, but he had joined the ARP. Along with her mother and grandmother they lived in a house that was well protected from the bombing:

Our house, like many others, had the lower windows at the back completely sand-bagged as a protection against bomb blast and my grandmother and I slept in the downstairs dining room against the inner walls.

In the event of an air-raid during the night — a frequent occurrence — my grandmother and I, as the oldest and youngest members of the household, would be hustled down to a neighbour's house where they had an indoor shelter. This was located in a downstairs room and was known as 'the battleship' shelter. We sat in this protected area in comparative comfort with a couple of old dears from the neighbourhood drinking tea, eating biscuits, knitting, sewing and generally discussing the destruction being wrought all around us.

During these sojourns in the shelter it was customary for my mother, in deference to my grandmother's wishes, to wear on her head an old handle-less saucepan stuffed with a scarf. As a measure of protection against shrapnel it was worse than useless, but it pleased and reassured the old lady. It was also a source of comic amusement, the anxious face beneath the adornment emphasising the absurdity of the device, but it helped morale no end. The toddler next door observed, 'I've seen soldiers with khaki tin hats, my daddy has an air force blue one, but I have never seen a silver one before.'

Sheilah Freeman remembers living in a small village outside of Exeter, in the south west of England. At 8 a.m. a German bomber came sweeping out of the sky and dropped a bomb that hit the house and completely destroyed one wall:

My landlady was so annoyed that she forgot all about her safety and ran into the road shaking her fist up at the bomber, saying, 'You bastard! We haven't even finished paying for that house yet.'

Olive Oatridge lived in the Rhondda, South Wales. Surely one of the safest places in Britain, hadn't many of the evacuees been sent to this area?

9th October, 1940. The day that was to change my life completely. Until that day I was part of a God-fearing, happy Welsh family. In fact we were told that air-raid shelters would not be necessary as the mountains would shield us from enemy attacks.

However, on the morning of the 9th, my mother realising that something was worrying me, made me promise that when I returned home that evening I would tell her of my worries.

I hurried home. My mother forgot to ask me, instead I was reproached for being home late.

A lone German plane was being chased over the valley after a raid on Swansea and to accelerate his speed the pilot decided to drop the bombs he was carrying as quickly as possible. The plane carried three bombs, two of which fell on the mountainside and the third was a direct hit on my home.

The house rocked and crumbled, walls and ceilings fell around us and the noise was deafening. Patricia, our evacuee, and I were buried under the piano. Olive, a visiting friend, protected her head from falling masonry. I called out to my mother, but there was no answer.

How long we lay there I can't remember, but suddenly there was a sweet smell of gas and with it a feeling of wanting to sleep. Everything was so peaceful. The rain started falling and I wondered why it was possible to feel the rain in my home. Sleep was so near. Then a voice called out, 'Is there anybody there?' I whispered to Patricia to keep quiet but being only four she was very frightened and screamed aloud. ARP workers were scrambling over the debris to get to us as quickly as possible because of the escaping gas.

My mother was both house-proud and fastidious and all I could find to say was how furious she would be to see people walking all over her furniture.

Little did I know that my mother, or Mam as she was known to us, was dead.

God works in a mysterious way; he answered my prayers and Mam died without me having to tell her of my deep anxiety and dread that I feared she would soon die.

D. Bispham (now Mrs Manley) was ten and lived with her parents and three sisters in Plymouth, Devon. She continued to attend school despite the air-raids. Eventually a garden in a large square beside some expensive homes was dug up and an underground shelter was installed:

My father survived the horrors of Dunkirk and when he at last came home on leave he tried to describe how terrible mass bombing and fire incendiary bombs had been. He was horrified to find out where we were sheltering because he realised how vulnerable this type of concrete tube could be if it received a direct hit. Father arranged with the church warden at the church near our house for the family to share the cellar of the church with his family.

My brother was born during one of the worst raids and the midwife had a difficult job to reach the house because there was an unexploded bomb in the lane near the house. She persuaded the ARP to help her to clamber over piles of rubble and she arrived in time to deliver the baby. My mother had to get up from bed almost immediately to go to the church cellar because another raid had begun.

Millicent Bransom recalls that she was ten when the war started and was living in the Isle of Wight. She was on a family visit to Portsmouth with her two sisters when the warning sirens began to wail:

As we crowded into the shelter together with our aunt, uncle and cousin, it was soon apparent that this was a more than usually heavy raid. Whenever my uncle removed the door of the shelter the sky glowed an angry red and the noise was almost as bad as Dad had always warned us to expect.

Uncle and Dad made frequent sorties above ground to check that no incendiaries had caught the house.

It was not until years later that they revealed that they had spotted a stationary ammunition train on the main London–Portsmouth railway line that ran the other side of the garden wall — literally only yards from the shelter! I can clearly remember my mother agonising that she had left our three new winter coats upstairs and every time Uncle ventured out Auntie would say, 'Put the kettle on for a cup of tea, Jack.' Uncle's reply was unprintable.

Both Irene Arnold and her husband were working in hospitals when the Germans bombed Portsmouth:

All our staff were incredibly busy when a lovely Hampshire voice said, 'The b—— might have knocked off a hell of a lot of 'em outside but he isn't upsetting our ward or stopping us having our tea break.'

As she, our faithful orderly, had stated, he thankfully didn't and we all were ready for the 'next round'.

But sadly he got her on her way home.

Although Bristol had experienced air-raids, it was not until the last weeks of November that the city felt the full force of a Luftwaffe attack. Olive James (now Perry) was fourteen and living with her family in the southern part of the city:

Every night we were out of our beds and under the stairs, Kath, my stepmother, nursing her baby in her arms. On one of these raids my gran's house next door was alight, her bedroom burned out by incendiaries and the neighbours formed a bucket chain which saved the rest of the house and the block of houses.

Dad was on fire watch and, when the raids got really bad, shouted to my sister and myself to get up and keep away from the windows as shrapnel was falling like rain. The noise was the thing I remember. The guns pounding, and mobile guns going up and down the road. Then a cheer would be heard and a call to see the German plane that had been hit, smoke trailing as it plunged to the ground.

Dad came in on one night when he was on fire watch and told us a young man just married had been killed by a bomb blast. He had laid in the road when he heard the stick of bombs coming down, instead of the grass verge where Dad and others were, and had died without a mark on him.

The Anderson shelters were put in the back gardens now and Dad put wooden bunks and duck boards on the concrete floor with an oil-lamp for lighting. It all looked cosy.

One night he came running up the stairs telling us the raid was getting bad and we must get up and go into the Anderson shelter. We looked in, but with Dad and Kath and the baby there wasn't much room. We went into the garden next door and lifted the sack across the opening. Gran and Uncle Bill were sitting in deck-chairs with the frost glistening on the floor.

This was enough for us and we decided then and there that we would take our chances under the stairs or sit by the fire grate in our easy chairs and we never went into an Anderson shelter again.

I was visiting my maternal grandmother in Bristol when a major raid started. I was ready to get the 6 p.m. bus into the centre of Bristol when Gran asked me to get the next bus and stop and talk for a while. The sirens went between 6 p.m. and half-past six, the buses stopped running and I had to stay at Gran's.

As the night wore on, things got worse. There were bombs falling all around. My uncle George, who had been in the First World War, was in and out of the house talking to the fire watch and ARP and coming indoors to tell us of the latest direct hits. The noise was terrific and Gran gave me some cotton wool to put in my ears. Purdown Percy, the huge gun, was firing most of the time and adding to the noise of the explosions from the bombs.

The all clear sounded in the early hours of the morning. Uncle walked me into town as it was a Monday and my job at the tobacco factory was near the centre. When we walked along the cut and under the underpass of Temple Meads Station we came into Victoria Street. What I saw was devastating. Buildings burning, factories just a mass of twisted girders with walls collapsing and water and gas pipes fractured. Fire hoses all over the road. Temple Church was blazing with long flames reaching right through the fallen roof. I wondered if the factory had been hit, as we neared the rear entrance, with shouts from the firemen to stay clear of walls and unexploded bombs. There was a crater in the road caused by a land mine. Most of the buildings were gutted by fire. The factory was somehow intact except for broken windows and the electricity cut off.

The Bristol I knew, Castle Street, Old Market, was gone overnight, but St Mary Redcliff stood out against the rubble and burnt-out shops. One chemist shop had the plate glass blown out, but the glass shelves still had bottles of perfume and medicines undamaged.

The dray horses at George's Brewery were injured and no-one could get to them because of the damage. Their cries were pitiful to hear.

I feel that Gran's asking me to get the next bus saved my life, as I would have been caught in the target area when walking from Old Market to my bus at Princess Street.

Dad found the fin of an incendiary bomb in the cavity wall, causing a damp patch. He also had a new toilet pan fitted in the bathroom as a stray bomb dropped in front of the house, causing a pavement slab to crash through the roof and smash the pan in half. As Dad said with a smile, 'Good job nobody was sat on it at the time.'

Mary Chamberlain (now Constance) was sixteen. Her father owned a Bristol cinema and although the sirens went often enough they had yet to construct a shelter:

This was to be the woodshed and coal cellar which faced you as you came down a flight of concrete steps from the kitchen into

Above: Young children, evacuated from London, practise wearing gas-masks at their new school.

Below: A warden fits one of the special 'Mickey Mouse' respirators made in bright colours for children.

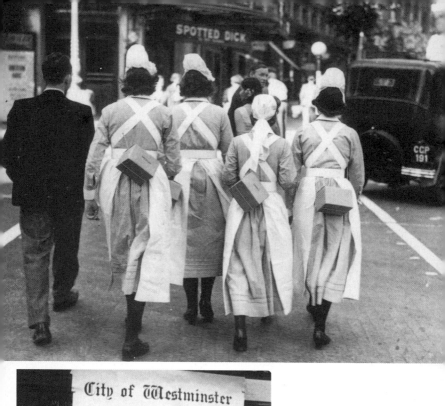

SPOTTED DICK

CCP 191

City of Westminster

AIR RAID PRECAUTIONS

GAS MASK FITTING CENTRE

for all persons (men. women and children) residing in the City of Westminster. except children under 5 years of age for whom other arrangements are being made.

PARKER MORRIS,
Town Clerk

September, 1938.

WAY IN »»»

CO.

Above: Hospital nurses with gas-masks added to their uniforms, September 1939.

Left: Even before the outbreak of war, Londoners were advised to take precautions.

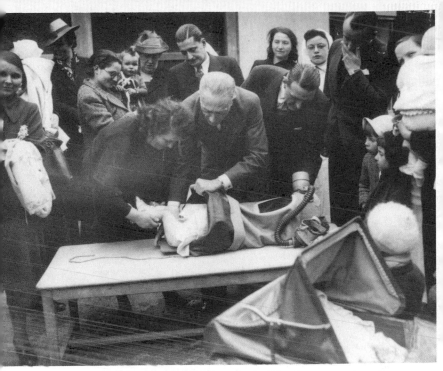

Above: The inventor of a gas-mask for infants, Dr Le Mée, demonstrates how to use the protective sack.
Below: Women air-raid wardens snatch a conversation with soldiers on an exercise in Kent.

Air-raid shelters being delivered to residents in Islington, London, 1939.

As soon as war was declared, people had to learn how to black out their windows and prevent the glass from splintering by sticking brown paper across the panes.

Above: Helping soldiers to fill sandbags, which were essential for strengthening buildings and gave additional protection during bomb attacks.

Below: Londoners queue with their bedding outside the city's first deep shelter, July 1944.

Above: The dramatic scene of St Paul's Cathedral in the blitz.

Below: A searchlight being manned by an ATS girl during a night alert.

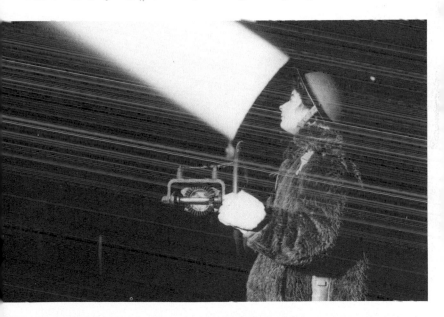

Becoming accustomed to using Underground stations at night, people found ingenious means of making themselves as comfortable as possible, from hammocks slung between the rails to bunk beds on the platform.

Children were well catered for in the shelters, which could double as a café or a playground.

Left: St John's nurses in attendance at Piccadilly Underground station.

Below: Larger and better-equipped shelters were built in London as the war progressed. This one, at Liverpool Street Underground station, could accommodate a thousand people. Here, a concert is in progress in one of the recreation rooms.

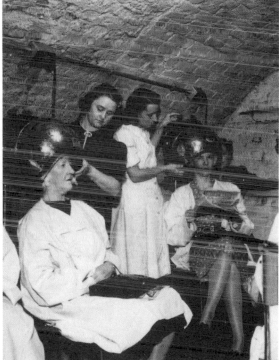

Sheltering underground
became part of everyday life.
Employees of Marks and
Spencer, above, have
transferred their canteen
below ground, while for a
London hairdressing salon,
right, it is business as usual.

Young and old prepare to
settle down for a long night in
the shelters.

A scene of devastation in London's Oxford Street, where firemen turn their hoses on a blaze at John Lewis.

After a raid, wardens and residents would salvage what they could from the rubble. Sometimes there were lucky finds—like the mirror, below, that did not break!

Rescuers often placed themselves at great risk, entering precarious bomb-damaged homes in search of survivors.

All hands on deck: clearing up after a raid could be a time-consuming business.

the large reinforced cellar that formed the foundations of our house. But for the time being we were to use a room under the main stairs in the cinema.

At first we thought it was fun. If the sirens went in the daytime (invariably at meal times), we would all march out, complete with plates of food, round the back of the house which with two shops and the cinema formed a block of buildings. We would go in through the back door and up the outside steps which led to the operating room and eventually into this little room under the stairs. If the raid was likely to come that night we would don siren-suits. My sister always seemed very brave and well organised (she made sure the hangers in the wardrobe all faced the same way to enable us to remove the clothes quickly — a practice I maintain to this day!).

I, however, was scared stiff from my first realisation that this nightly ritual might go on for a long time.

The fun soon wore off. One night I had an outburst of hysteria. I cannot remember what it was about — I imagine the pent-up frustrations of my sixteen years, the frequent broken nights, the impossibility of trying to work at school with constant movements to and from the shelter, the strangeness and different kind of life we were living, all contributed to this final outburst. My mother was angry and told me to get out of the shelter. I felt at the time it was the utmost cruelty. Only later did I realise the strain she must have been under. But where could I go? Out into the fearful darkness of the night where I might be bombed, or into the silent, impenetrable darkness of the city with its celluloid ghosts.

I took the only other course. This was the lavatory opposite the shelter. And there I screamed and screamed until I was exhausted, feeling very frightened and very much alone.

On the last night we were ever in the shelter, we awoke as usual for our tea and biscuits, then settled down for what we hoped would be a peaceful night. It was my mother who first noticed what was happening and it must have been her exclamation that woke us up. In the glow of the night light we watched as a family of mice scuttled around the legs of our bunks, enjoying the feast of biscuit crumbs we had dropped. 'That's it!' said my mother.

'Hitler can come and bomb us at home. This is positively the last night I spend in here!'

The cinema shelter had no windows, of course, but there was a ventilation shaft. Should the cinema collapse around us, it would be possible to crawl through this and out through an opening in the outside wall on to the stairs leading from the operating box. When my mother realised where the mice were coming from she made a firm stand. Neither Hitler nor anyone else was going to make her crawl through that shaft, past a row of thickly dust-encrusted pipes and generations of mice.

I do not remember exactly when we moved into our finally completed cellar shelter. I think it must have been the first time we had a real raid. Father had fixed up a very tiny emergency electric light. The first stick of bombs fell, cut off the power and blew away the small curtain that covered the one small window. Father decided that he had better not switch on his light. Through the window we could see a great red glow.

'Good God, Roy,' exclaimed Mother. 'D'you really think with all that hell going on out there they're going to see that miserable bulb? Switch it on!' But for some reason it wouldn't work and it never did.

Wendy Gibbs was living in Bristol when the sirens went. She, her mother and four sisters headed for the Anderson shelter at the bottom of their garden.

Next door they were rather posh, so they had a brick shelter made.

My father was in the Home Guard, so had not joined us in our shelter. We were all awake as we couldn't sleep and suddenly we heard this plane. Mum said, 'It's a bloody plane coming down.' We all got up and tore back the curtains on the shelter door to look. It was not only a plane coming down but a parachute too. As he floated down he got closer and closer and suddenly landed on the roof of the brick shelter next door.

It was a German pilot, so my mother said, 'There's nobody about, so I suppose I'll have to do it.' She grabbed a pitchfork and a broom and marched out to the garden next door and stood at the bottom of the shelter and, facing the pilot, said in a loud voice, 'You're under arrest. Put your hands up!' She was fantastic. So he surrendered to my mother and gave her his parachute. She quickly threw it into the shelter before the Home Guard came to take him away.

The next day she dyed the chute yellow and two weeks later two little girls went off to school dressed in bright yellow dresses.

The future Mrs Mary Birch was thirteen in November, 1940 and washing up the dishes at her home in Bristol:

As the siren started, I went to say, 'Oh, no, not again,' when all hell broke loose. We shot under the stairs, followed smartly by the cat, and remained there until the all clear.

I lived on the outskirts of the city and my route went mainly past quiet fields. School was almost empty. There were about three boys and myself in my class. No work was done until we had history with the senior mistress last lesson. She demanded our homework. Mine had been done on Friday under Mother's eagle eye. The boys tried to slide out of it, saying, 'There was a blitz!'

It didn't wash.

'That was Sunday,' she said – and they stayed on detention to get it done.

Gwen Adams recalls living in Bristol with her mother, three-year-old brother and two aunts who were getting away from the London bombing:

The night of 24th November was the first big blitz on Bristol, when most of the centre area was wiped out. We went to bed to be woken by air-raid wardens about one hour later to say that we had an unexploded bomb in the road outside. We dressed quickly and set off walking to a school about two miles away, where there were hundreds of others who had been bombed out. My brother and I found a corner of floor while my mother and aunts set to helping with food and drink. In the morning we went outside and walked towards the Bedminster area, passing some houses where some ladies were at their gates talking.

One lady asked what we were doing. Obviously my mother must have explained. This lady (I do not remember her name) said come in and use my front room for as long as you want it. We stayed there for four days while the bomb near our house was dealt with. It sums up the spirit of the times. Strangers who helped out other strangers.

Joyce Angerstein (now Smith) was ten and in hospital in Bath, having her tonsils removed:

The sirens sounded and at first none of the staff or children in the ward seemed to be very frightened. The aircraft noises and bombing came much closer and suddenly there was a mighty explosion in the grounds of the hospital and the glass walls of the ward shattered and we were left in the open air. The nurses very quickly put several of us into one big iron hospital cot and wheeled us to a lift where we were taken to a new and very crowded ward. Two or three other cots followed us into the ward. All night long while the bombing continued and the overworked nurses attended to the patients, I amazed the twin toddlers who were placed in the cot with me. I sang to them, played 'Walkie round the garden', 'This little piggy' and told them stories until morning.

My father drove a furniture van that could be used as an ARP ambulance, so when he heard about the bombing he put up his ambulance sign and drove the thirteen miles to Bath, being allowed through restricted areas because of his 'ambulance'. He collected me from the hospital and although I was not due for discharge, I was allowed to go home. The nurses were full of praise for his 'courageous little girl', but my nervous system paid a high price for this during the following months.

Two things I shall never forget about that journey home are the shattered homes and weary dirty people scratching for belongings or relatives, and the fact that my father had managed to get some chocolate for me and I was unable to eat it because of my swollen sore throat.

Geoffrey Clappison and his parents had been living with friends until it was safe for them to return to their home in Hull:

When we returned home there was some damage to the house with windows smashed. Amazingly enough our pet budgie was still alive and chirping, despite his cage having been blown to the floor and deposited under the table.

With their steeples standing out like beacons, churches attracted many of the bombs. Alex Crawford was an apprentice joiner during the Glasgow and Clydebank blitz. He found himself running back and forth with timber, shoring up buildings to assist rescue crews:

On this particular occasion I travelled from our workplace in Govan to Clydebank, a distance of about four miles, to Kilbowie Road. I was horrified at the sight which met me. There was hardly a building left standing, but in the midst of all this chaos was Radnor Park Church and it was a joiner and myself's job to shore up the pillars from the balcony to the roof, which had been knocked off plumb with the blast, and there was a danger of the roof falling in.

We did manage to shore up each pillar, plumb it and then lower it back in place.

The main thing that struck me was that there were hundreds of incendiary bombs lying in the seats. Two were even on a soft seat in the minister's vestry, but it was the only building in the whole area that did not burn.

Eileen Paterson was the youngest of four and remembers being in the wash-house at the back of her Clydebank home when the windows came in. Her mother lay over her and her sister to protect her. Later when the house caught fire she was carried in a blanket along the street:

Everything seemed to be on fire. All the windows of tenement buildings nearby. John Brown's wood yard blazing.

Dad and brother passed each other on the stairs when blown in opposite directions. Brother out in Montrose Street giving stray cat milk as bombs fell. Mum cross when incendiary bomb landed on wardrobe and was put out with precious sack of flour and warm water from someone's greenhouse. (Flour and paste everywhere.)

Two goats found sitting in armchairs when man searching houses for survivors. Food lorry came to give sandwiches — Mum kept this food till correct meal-time.

We were taking wood from round football-pitch when two policemen appeared. Dad said, 'Just carry on,' but we were shaking. Policemen came and helped gather the wood and board up where the windows had been. Really very helpful.

Mrs M. Pennock arrived back at her home in Swansea, south Wales, after spending an evening walking with friends. The siren went and they took shelter under the Guildhall for the night:

When I eventually got to our street I could see straight away that our house had had a direct hit. Only my mother and brother were there. Luckily they went to the Anderson shelter. My mother tried to shield my brother when the bomb fell and had some shrapnel in her back which nearly pierced her lung. It was never removed and caused her death in the end. I was lucky in a way, because I would never go to the shelter and most of the roof of the house and rafters etc fell on the bed in my room.

Anyway, the wardens took me to the house where most of the survivors were all crammed in one room. My mother and my brother were there with a lot of bombed-out people and in the far corner was a friend of ours who had gone into labour and was having her baby. It was all such a nightmare. I had only got married in the July, so I not only lost my home and nearly lost my family, but I lost all my wedding presents, clothes, the lot, but was so thankful that my mother and brother were saved.

Betty Baxter was also living in Swansea, and visiting a sister who had given birth to a baby that day:

They kept a hotel, so we carried her downstairs, went to the bar and all buried our heads under the bench seats. I don't know why, but we felt we were safer by doing that. We hadn't got used to the shelter at that time.

A favourite uncle was taken short with shock. He was in the outdoor loo when another bomb was whistling down. He came running in and you've heard the saying, 'Never let your braces dangle', well, that happened to Uncle and we weren't sure if we preferred the bombs to his company.

In the face of the horrific there is always humour. G. Davies lived in Liverpool, close to the docks, and had come through a fierce week-end's bombing:

On the Monday I went to the Co-Op grocer's and was shocked to see the front blown away. A customer passed comment, 'How awful,' and with typical Liverpool wit an assistant said, 'You should see our Berlin branch.'

It's easy to look on the time of the blitz as one when everyone was kind, considerate and went out of the way to help neighbours. However, goods suddenly lying around unclaimed proved too much of a temptation for some.
   Peggy Parker had three small children and was bombed out in December, 1940:

We all saved and got the children their Christmas presents and the looters came in the night and took everything. It was heart-breaking because we could not afford any more. Their fingers should have dropped off, but they done it to most houses, not only mine.

Henry Barnes was home on leave from the RAF during a heavy raid on Hull in the north east. His father's grocery and off-licence was completely destroyed:

As soon as daylight dawned, the inevitable happened — looters! A policeman was sent to guard the goods and this PC turned out to be the father of the girl I was married to. My own mother and father came to our house at 3 a.m. and found us crouching in the Anderson shelter. Their first words were, 'We've lost everything. All we have are the few clothes we are wearing.'
   As daylight came my father said, 'Will you go to the shop and see if you can rescue the cash?' I knew where the cash-bags were kept — in a fixture no more than about three feet from the ground.

I arrived to find this bit of wall still standing. I moved some rubble, managed to get my hand into the fixture and there it was. Intact! Every penny (looters failed).

Connie Brown (now Blunsum) had been out to an ARP lecture and returned home at about 8.45 p.m. when the siren sounded:

We could not have an Anderson shelter because we were a corner house. About 9 p.m. a 500 lb bomb fell in the back garden and we were all buried under the debris until about 5.30 a.m. the next day.

I remember a noise like a train rattling down, then a shrill whistle and a bang, then we went up in the air and down again. I did not lose consciousness and was covered by brickwork, etc, and pinned down by a dining chair which had lost its seat and was over my shoulders.

My house was a complete loss and the houses either side were in various stages of demolition. Four people were killed and nineteen injured. My father was a policeman on war reserve, as was our next door neighbour. The neighbour and his wife were found dead at their meal table.

The people in the downstairs flat had just brought their daughter home from Exeter, where she had been evacuated. She went to lie down for a rest and her body was found the next day. The fourth death was a young baby from the upper flat next door whose mother flung herself over the cradle to protect her. The mother suffered two broken legs. The baby died.

I can remember the sounds of men digging and then calling to us after what seemed ages. The strange thing is you make all sorts of promises to God if one could get out alive, and then accept that you are probably going to die. When the rescue gang got nearer they told us to cover our heads. I put my arms up and a brick smashed my elbow and my face and hair were covered in glass. The gentleman from the ground floor was injured beside me, but we couldn't move to help each other. Then the rescuers said that they were going to lower flasks of water on a rope. I managed to catch one but could not get my head back to drink because the back of the chair which entrapped me made putting my head back impossible.

Eventually I was released and, to add insult to injury, the man assisting me said, 'You will be all right now, son.' Not very flattering for a nineteen-year-old girl.

We lost our home and all our belongings. The hundredweight of coal got in for the winter was looted along with some unbroken movable objects and clothing.

Barbara Grant worked in a shoe shop in London:

The shelter we customarily used was full so we went to another. This turned out to be fortunate as our usual shelter received a direct hit, killing a number of shop assistants and customers.

There was another raid on the Monday night again, with the sirens sounding about eight o'clock. This time, my parents, sister and I were quickly down to our Anderson shelter in the garden, trying to get some sleep, when round midnight the house was struck by a bomb.

All we knew about it was when the building fell on us and we were buried beneath the rubble. We were, however, unhurt and shortly after the wardens and rescue services were heard calling through the debris, 'Are you all right? We'll soon have you out,' although it was about dawn before we clambered out to see the devastation caused to our house. It had been virtually split in half and was quite uninhabitable.

The emergency services seemed to be swamped. We were asked if we had anywhere to go. My eldest brother lived at Slough in Bucks and my father thought it best that we try to go there. So, with nothing but the clothes we stood in, we wended our way towards the station. On the way, we must have looked like refugees, which we were, and somewhere *en route* a very genteel lady from one of the big houses asked if we had been bombed out, took us in and gave us hot drinks. She then fed us and insisted that we all went to bed to recover well enough to travel.

We went on to Slough. A few days later my father and I returned to Lewisham to see what we could salvage of our belongings. The building was unsafe and they would not allow other than the most perfunctory of searches — although we managed to find a few documents and light household goods. Remarkably, however, someone had managed to get in, because everything of value, including bedding and furniture, had been looted. We were numb with sorrow and hung on to each other and cried.

In contrast to the lady who was so kind, we also remember that not all Londoners were so honourable and willing to help the unfortunate.

Mary Richards lived with her parents close to Coventry and after constant air-raids her father decided that it would be a good idea to visit relatives in the small town of Bedworth for a few days:

As luck would have it, we went to stay with them the very night before the 1940 blitz on Coventry. The next night we were awoken by a dreadful noise of German aircraft passing over.

Two days after this blitz, my elder brother and some friends went over to our Coventry home on their bikes to try and bring back some of our possessions and to find out the extent of the damage. Well, the house had lost its roof, all the windows had gone, all the ceilings were down and the furniture damaged and pottery all smashed.

I remember the one thing that hurt my mother the most was that someone (who was very expert) had entered our house and taken about two feet of beading off the front of her sideboard. It had been done very neatly, but she never understood why they didn't take it all. It grieved her all her life that her sideboard had been spoilt.

A lot of looting had already taken place by this time and many of my clothes, toys and our household possessions had been taken. At this stage of my life I couldn't believe that others would enter someone else's house and take things away.

9

'The Most Unusual Christmas I Can Ever Remember'

Weather conditions during the beginning of December forced many of the German bombers to stay home. For a while, raids ceased to be a nightly occurrence.

Yet still the German planes found time for London. The air attacks continued, leaving houses in some areas flattened, with piles of bricks to form the new playgrounds for the local children. Those houses that remained standing in the bombed locations suffered from shortages of gas and water as burst mains spilt their contents along the glass-covered roads. Many could be seen each morning salvaging what little they could and piling it on carts before wheeling it off to friends, neighbours or local rest centres.

Some idea of the help needed can be seen by a study of figures which show that an incredible 250,000 Londoners had been made homeless by the bombing before the end of October, 1940. After one particularly heavy night of bombing, one-fifth of the homes in the London area were without gas or water.

To add to the problems of the sufferers was the frustration of dealing with the bureaucratic mind when asking for help. Even when improvements were approved they seemed to take forever to be implemented.

By the end of November the Treasury had finally agreed to help with the cost of looking after the homeless. The armed services and industry were diverted to give assistance where needed in the capital. Efforts were made to improve the living conditions in the shelters by introducing electric light and toilet facilities.

The German bombers had a new form of navigation aid, a system of special transmitters which sent radio beams across to England until the sound in the earphones signalled that they were over the target. In the attacks on London this was hardly necessary, however: the city could be seen for miles as the sky glowed with the leaping flames and the beams of searchlights rocking back and forth.

The various noises that could be heard during an air-raid encouraged all manner of guesses as to what the newest make of weapon being used by the Germans might be.

Monica Harris (now O'Brian)'s young brother kept white mice:

During a particularly heavy raid they escaped when their cage door broke open during the blast.

Our family was in the Anderson shelter when suddenly these little white creatures were running down the shelter.

'My God!' said my mum. 'Now they're dropping white mice!'

K. F. Dobson lived with his parents in Essex. At the height of the blitz the Germans had hit the oil tanks at Purfleet, just a few miles down the road:

My mum was so scared that she wouldn't let my dad report for Home Guard duty. Eventually his commanding officer came around to the house to find where he was. We were all down the shelter in the garden. The commanding officer told my dad he would have to go, as they were expecting to be invaded that night.

Mum was crying for him not to leave us, so Dad said, 'Look. I've got a bottle of whisky indoors. I'll leave that with you, Eileen, and every time a bomb drops close, you have a swig of whisky.'

So off he went with the officer. Well, in the morning about 7 a.m. Dad popped his head in the shelter doorway and said, 'Are you all right, Eileen? Let's have a swig of whisky, I've had a hell of a night.'

Mum pointed to the empty whisky bottle and said, 'I don't care if Hitler himself walks in here.' She was as drunk as a lord.

Peggy Hickson had spent nearly a year driving a double-decker bus converted into a mobile canteen for the National Fire Service in London. She remembers the sinking of the Marchioness *at Southwark Bridge:*

We had been alerted to go to a big fire near the bridge and I had to park the bus as near to the water as possible. To our horror we could see a land mine caught by its white parachute on one of the iron pikes swaying gently backwards and forwards. We were all terrified that it would hit the bridge. The bomb-disposal men did a superb job detonating it and eventually we were sent to Warren Street that was being bombed.

The courage of the firemen was fantastic. Never complaining and giving us a cheer when we arrived. In the early morning, returning to the fire station, driving through the streets of London to be flagged down by City gents waving umbrellas thinking it was their bus to get to work was very funny, especially since I am only five feet four and in those days weighed only seven stone and had to sit on cushions to see over the driving wheel.

Elsie Swann was living with her parents in north London during the bombing raids of 1940. Every night she would dash home from the office, eat a meal, get washed and changed into pyjamas, slacks and jumper, ready for the night:

For those three months my mother and I slept on a bed made up on the floor underneath the staircase of our house and my two sisters slept underneath a heavy billiard table. My father, who was a veteran of three major battles in the First World War, insisted on sleeping upstairs.

Sometimes the raids were so long, the all clear had not sounded when it was time to go to work the next morning, but nobody ever thought of being late for work.

Ernest Otto was working at the Vauxhall Motors plant in Luton, assembling Churchill tanks:

While at work a single German plane dropped a parachute mine which crashed through the roof of the hangar and was suspended by the cords caught on the beams, leaving it hanging nine feet from the floor. It was not long before a team of men came to make the mine safe. This meant moving the mine to get at the fuses, which were two. During this task the mine fell the nine feet to the concrete floor. Lucky it did not explode.

Dorothy Hicks was working as a telephonist in the House of Commons:

Our switchboard was at the top of one of the turret towers. In my lunch break I was standing by the window when a stray enemy fighter plane made a dashing run for it up the Thames. Thinking it was one of ours, I opened the window wide to cheer him on. He opened fire on me!

Henry Baggott was out fire-watching:

The Germans had been dropping bombs for quite a while when suddenly flares were dropped directly above. I looked around but could not see any of the others, so I went to a brick-built shelter where we kept our equipment for dealing with incendiary bombs they may drop. I pushed the door open and found the other men inside. One of the men said, 'Come in quick.' Just as I said 'No' I heard the whine of a bomb falling. I dropped between both shelters, kept my chest off the ground and breathed through my teeth. Then from the corner of my right eye I saw a shower of sparks and heard a grinding noise. Everything seemed to be hitting me. Then I found myself buried up to my thighs in the crater. The men in the shelter, including a fourteen-year-old, were all killed.

Doris Collier (now Jaye) had returned to London after being evacuated. She was fourteen and with her father watched a German aircraft being shot down:

My father and I ran to have a look. I pulled on my slacks but in my haste they were back to front, so I ran down the road holding my trousers up. I was most disappointed at only seeing a pair of flying boots, as we hated the Germans so much I wanted to see a body.

Honor Kenyon (now Price) was a school teacher who lived close to Marble Arch:

A whole block of evacuated old homes in Eastbourne Terrace, running along the west side of Paddington Station, had been turned into a hostel for ranks of all the services where they could get a good meal and bed for a very small sum.

The hostel was manned by volunteer workers and my stretch was from 10 p.m. to 2 a.m. each day. After a particularly bad night and full day's work I felt so tired that I rang the supervisor and cried off for one night.

That night, at about 1 a.m., a land mine dropped in Eastbourne Terrace and destroyed the entire block.

I then joined the staff of an officers' club in Westminster. One day Clark Gable arrived for a meal and sat at one of the tables. He sat down and immediately produced a comb and combed his hair.

Kitty Steel lived in London and served the first year of the war as a nurse in a health clinic that acted as an air-raid shelter. As there were no air-raids she asked to transfer to the buses:

Well, the pay for nurses was £2-10-0 and a bus conductor £4-18-0. My daughter was expecting her first baby and decided to go to Scotland and stay with her husband's mother.

We received a letter from the Lewisham Council that if she did not come back to occupy the house she had left they would take it back for people who had been bombed out. So she came back. One night the warning went and a bomb dropped next door.

Fortunately my daughter was down below in a shelter. A neighbour called out, 'Are you all right, Molly?' and Molly said, 'Yes! My door key is under the front door mat.' The neighbour called back and said, 'Your front door is on top of your stairs, Molly.'

Betty Grant (now Wells) lived in Fulham with three aunts, a great-aunt and a sister:

Most nights during the blitz in our Anderson shelter my great-aunt was always coming home with gadgets to enable us to boil a kettle in the shelter. One day she brought home something resembling a cocoa tin with a night-light in it and we took it in turns to hold the kettle over it. I cannot remember what came first, the 'all clear' or the tea.

Eileen Horrocks lived and worked in London:

The city of London had been bombed mercilessly. After one particularly bad night, morning at last dawned.

Arriving at the entrance of Debenham and Freebody where I worked in the basement office, I was very moved to see our office cleaner on her knees washing the small-paned glass pavement lights.

As the Christmas season approached, the black-out seemed even more restrictive. People who could remember the decorations before the war exaggerated in their mind's eye how gaily lit the city had been. The cinema was still very popular, though most people went in the afternoons to enable them to get home before the black-out. But losing oneself in a film was only a temporary escape from reality. Mary Moss (now Scott) had booked to go to the Gaumont to see a charity concert just before Christmas. She kept a diary at that time that reads:

Sunday 22nd Dec. We went to Gaumont to see Harry Fryer and his Orchestra. Just started when incendiary bomb fell through (on to the stage) curtains on fire, copper works, paper mill. Came home in it and Joan stayed the night until all clear.

I've never forgotten that Sunday night. The incendiary bomb came down and the curtains caught fire. The manager was in one of the circle boxes directing the stirrup-pump down and then the safety curtain was lowered. Stanley Tudor started playing the organ and everyone joined in. There was no panic. We were all led out to a brick air-raid shelter.

I decided to try and walk home. The planes came back and gunfire was heavy. As usual, the bombers seemed to be following the river. There was a factory on the corner and we thought we would shelter there. There was a night watchman in there who seemed to be alone. I think he was pleased to see us. He had an old round iron fire, glowing with red cinders, and he gave us a cup of tea.

After about an hour (we sat and talked together and told him how bad things were out there), we decided it had quietened down a little and we decided to try and get home.

It was hop, skip and jump and shelter, and then we ran. We used to go down the cellar belonging to the family opposite and the raid was still on.

I called out, 'Let us in, quickly!' They helped us down. They were all relieved to see us, but my friend couldn't get home until the morning. Her parents were frantic — none of us had telephones and I don't think they would have worked anyway.

When morning and daylight came, I said I would walk home with my friend. We had to do a detour because the short cut, an iron bridge over the river, was useless. The bridge and everywhere was bomb-damaged. That meant we had to pass the factory corner where we had sheltered during the night.

We couldn't believe it — the factory corner where we were had had a direct hit and it was all in the river. I couldn't help feeling very sad about the night watchman.

Joe Goodwin also went to the theatre in December, 1940, four miles out of Sheffield. Henry Hall and his dance band were making an appearance at the Empire:

We had hardly settled into our seats when an announcement heralded the news of an air-raid warning alert. Not long after, Henry Hall asked us to leave as events were getting hectic. On reaching the street, by the back entrance, the windows of shops were already reflecting fires burning. The scream of falling bombs put us to flight.

Off we raced hell for leather. Coming to a ramp, down to a garage under a building. Like two jack rabbits down a bolt hole, at break-neck speed, scattering people looking out.

Peering out during a lull, I glanced up to see a face outlined above and filtering plumes of smoke. Hardly had I voiced my opinion, the place was on fire, when an air-raid warden appeared. 'First ten follow me,' he retorted. As the group retreated before our eyes the anti-aircraft guns around the city opened up. The warden's protégés ran amok in total panic amid screams of terror. He returned empty-handed, my friend and I volunteered to follow but do not remember many participants.

The guns had ceased by the time we reached the designated shelter through some double doors off the street, housing a car. We climbed up wooden steps to the top tier of a double shelter. I found a cubicle holding a sparkling new Elsan toilet and parked myself on the seat, much to my friend's amusement. In a hushed atmosphere the toilet gave a loud clank as I moved position, which caused the occupants to duck and cover their faces. Not the Hun, but that damn fellow on the loo.

There were long queues for Charlie Chaplin and The Great Dictator *at the Gaumont in the Haymarket and just across Leicester Square at the Empire, Judy Garland and Mickey Rooney were strutting their stuff in* Strike Up the Band. *For those who needed a good cry,* All This and Heaven, Too *with Bette Davis and Charles Boyer was at the Warner Cinema.*

There were twelve live shows in the West End, the most famous of them at the Windmill. It had adopted the slogan 'We Never Close' and attracted large numbers of servicemen on leave who needed to spend a relaxing hour watching scantily clad dancing girls.

The nightly attacks continued. More than 3000 incendiary bombs were dropped on 8th December alone, and again the emergency services scrambled to tackle the many fires. For many, it was a lonely Christmas: loved ones were far away, killed or maimed in the war that most had thought would be over long before now.

Betty Westwell had arrived back home in Salford, Lancashire, just before Christmas:

I had been going to stay with Elsie (a friend) overnight, but cancelled this as my brother was arriving home. This was to be the night it was 'our turn' and we were ensconced in our Anderson shelter as the bombers arrived. Elsie's house was hit and sadly, she died. After the all clear sounded, we were amazed to see that blast had blown all the windows out and killed our budgie in his cage. My brother was worried because he had not brought his Christmas presents — no-one realised the extent of the bombing and, incredibly looking back, my brother and I walked to Manchester, in awe at the damage.

Market Street was roped off and the firemen were still busy with hoses putting out fires. We thought this was quite exciting and seemed unaware of any danger. Shop windows were smashed and the contents were spewed on to the Market Street pavements. We were directed away from the main streets and eventually arrived at our destination — Lewis's — and were not at all surprised that the store was open: after all, the Christmas decorations and trees were there, so everything seemed all right.

When we arrived home, my father, who was a resourceful man, had taken up the 'lino' from the bedroom floors, made frames and covered the windows, creating total black-out.

Then next night saw us again in the shelter and this time things seemed worse. We lived near to the railway and Salford docks, so a direct hit was not improbable. We seemed to be in that shelter for hours and, during a quiet spell, my father dashed out to the house to fill the kettle. He flew back into the shelter with a look of disbelief on his face, then there was the loudest explosion I have ever heard — then uncanny silence. We afterwards discovered that what my father had seen sailing over our house was a land mine, which had scored a direct hit on the street behind ours and homes and lives were lost.

When we finally got back to the house, we discovered that the blast had blown out all the lino and my father said some very cryptic things about Hitler.

We had no gas, electricity or water — but we had each other and our house was intact. People who had lost their homes were streaming along the streets to be accommodated in church halls — I thought everyone was leaving except us.

My father was a member of the Home Guard and reported for duty to see what he could do to help. It turned out that the cemetery had been hit. He didn't tell us for a long time afterwards that they were collecting the scattered bones.

What a joy when he returned. He had been given a Christmas hamper containing large tins of chicken and ham and fruits and Christmas pudding. The lino was tacked back on the frames and so eliminated the draught from the open windows, and we ate our Christmas dinner by candlelight and gave out our presents. It was the most unusual Christmas I can ever remember.

The King decided to continue the tradition of delivering a Christmas message to his people, although his speech impediment made him uncomfortable in this role that his father had loved. But George VI soon began to weave a magic of his own, his stammer giving a force and sincerity to his broadcast. The King was stirring everyone to greater efforts as he talked of 'being in the front line together'.

If one bomb in the garden of Buckingham Palace made the King feel he was in the front line, the Christmas raids reinforced that idea. They had started during the night of 20th December, with an RAF raid on Berlin. Freight yards, railway stations and homes had shattered as British bombers pounded the city for several hours. Germany retaliated at once.

In the Paris headquarters of General Field Marshal Hugo Sperrle, Commanding General of Luftwaffe 3, heads were bent low over a large map of England. The word had arrived from the Fuhrer: London was to be hit as never before.

Hugo Sperrle was the Hollywood version of the perfect Teutonic villain, complete with monocle and short-cropped hair. He had been leading the raids on London since September and although he had not yet been able to force Churchill to negotiate a peace, he felt that the raid on Manchester a week earlier had been a great success. Thousands of fire bombs had blanketed the city and whole areas had been reduced to smouldering ruins. Why not direct the same kind of attack on London?

All agreed that the next raid would concentrate on the use of incendiary bombs, but it needed planning. First the weather had to be right. For more than a week, fog and overcast skies had restricted flying from the French airfields. The latest reports talked of an improvement, but there was also mention of an approaching storm front.

It was decided that 29th December was the ideal date. The position of the moon would mean abnormally low tides in the upper reaches of the Thames. Since this was where the London fire services would look for their water supplies, it was perfect timing for a fire raid.

The 29th was also a Sunday. The City of London, the business district, would be closed and most working people would be at home or in the country. Roof-spotters would still be enjoying the Christmas week and few would feel like spending time on the roofs of their offices. By the time the fire-watchers and roof-observers reached their posts, the damage would have been done.

The first planes over the target area would set the initial fires, lighting a path for those coming behind. One squadron of twenty bombers led by the much-decorated Hauptmann Friedrich Aschenbrenner was the obvious choice for the job. Aschenbrenner, a veteran of many bombing missions, had persuaded the authorities to give him only the best and most experienced of pilots and crew. They had quickly built a reputation throughout the German air force, earning the nickname the Fire Raisers.

As they left their base in Vanneson on the southern tip of Brittany and climbed towards the British coast, Aschenbrenner thought how much easier it would be to find the target than it had been in the earlier days. Now they had the X-apparatus, an almost foolproof electronic aid to navigation. Aschenbrenner glanced at his instrument panel. Altitude, 6,000 feet. Speed, 180 mph. He should be over the City of London at 6.08 p.m. He was.

10

Fire Over London

For London's firemen, 29th December was a night like no other. The first bombs fell in Southwark, close to London Bridge Station, and as the fire engines clanged their way through the flame-lit streets, the firemen had a better view than most of the approaching raiders. The whole sky seemed to be alive with falling incendiary bombs. Some were bouncing and spitting their flames along the pavements, but most had buried themselves deep in the timbers of the South Bank warehouses. Flames were leaping from one to the other. Although St Paul's remained unscathed, banks, offices, churches and houses all around were collapsing. The streets were piled high with charred rubble.

As firemen struggled against the worst of the blazes, they suddenly realised that the main water supply had been hit. No more than a trickle of water was coming from the hoses. In desperation, they headed for the Thames and waded through the mud of an exceptionally low tide in an attempt to reach the only water available. Soon an uncontrollable carpet of fire had spread around St Paul's.

Jean Dumpleton remembers she was twenty and living in Upper Norwood, south London:

We had an Anderson shelter which I did not like, having fears of being buried alive, but was forced to sleep in owing to more danger in my upstairs maisonette.

Life carried on and we managed to get to work somehow, undaunted and not to be beaten. A milkman gave me a lift one morning on his horse-drawn milk-cart as far as the Elephant and

Castle. Hilarious really, properly dressed for the City in a smart hat, gloves (in those days), a nice dress and very high-heel court shoes. Well, we had to keep the flag flying, didn't we?

Evenings during the winter months were one dash home from the office, trying to make it before the siren sounded. We had a very nice, friendly pub near to where I lived called the Rising Sun. It was kept by a middle-aged couple and to break the monotony of sitting in the Anderson shelter trying to read by night-light, we would spend part of some evenings there. I well remember a gin and lime at eightpence a glass.

If the flak got heavy (mobile gun batteries outside) and Jerry got rather too tiresome, the landlord would allow us to go down the cellar. Then we let rip with a sing-song.

I had a nasty piece of shrapnel come through the kitchen one evening when I had decided to try and get a proper meal; it came through the door at such speed and buried itself in the wall opposite. I had only just got up from the table to look at my rice pudding in the oven. The 'whizzing' sound was terrific and at the time I had no idea just what had happened, but as fright had taken place I dropped the almost cooked rice pudding on to the coconut matting, which took days to remove with a fork.

Looking back, I think 29th December, 1940 was our worst experience, when we all thought our beloved City of London would surely be completely devastated. It was a very dark night. I had just left the station. The train was late and the sirens sounded. I hurried, went into my local newsagent's for some cigarettes (hoping they could let me have ten), had a little chat and when I came out of the shop I just couldn't believe my eyes. I had never seen so many flares coming down from the skies before or since. It looked like fairyland.

I was fascinated. I was alone, everyone had beaten it home. I watched for a few seconds, realised that there were enemy aircraft overhead, realised my danger and ran hell-for-leather home.

I thought to myself, something is going to happen, we are in for a rough ride tonight. I made a flask of tea for the shelter as usual and as I made my way down the back stairs I noticed that the sky was particularly colourful, being a dark night, it looked rather vivid.

Neighbours nearby had gathered together in various shelters and I heard them all talking rather loudly. Being of a nosy nature at that point in time, wondering whether all was in order for the night vigil, I went to enquire. They were talking about London being on fire. News travelled fast by all accounts. I was told that 'if you go to the top of the hill you can see that the City is ablaze'. Well, although enemy aircraft were about, it wasn't too bad in our district at the time, so a few of us decided to go and see what all the commotion was about.

I have never forgotten that blazing sky. It was uncanny. It was all so red and vicious, you could see flames and smoke rising clearly into the darkness of the night. There were a lot of people at the top of the hill that night, but not for long. We heard high explosives being dropped, the vibration increased and then it seemed as though all hell had been let loose. We made a hasty retreat back to our shelters for the onslaught of the night.

I truly admit that was the most frightening night I can recall. My cat's eyes were like two yellow pools, large and bright. He no longer slept but literally leapt up towards my face suddenly, his tail swishing as he did so. He was scared and no mistake. The night-lights flickered, making patterns on the wavy ridges of the shelter walls. Bombs were raining down fast and furious now, one could hear the guns, they were firing at top speed, not far away. The noise was terrific. We were being bombarded. I was as scared as the cat. The shelter vibrated several times and I had visions of being buried alive in the thing.

When the raid eventually eased off and we all breathed a sigh of relief, I cannot remember whether I slept after that or not. I had tea from the flask. I could have done with a double brandy.

The cat slept peacefully, all was well, and we thanked God. I cannot remember the time the 'all clear' sounded and we struggled out of our shelters with our siren-suits, washed, cleaned our teeth, made some coffee and toast to begin the day once again. Everyone was talking about the raid on the station platform as we waited for the train. It was late. We all wondered whether we would be able to get to the City and we all felt shattered. I had noticed a few buildings which had 'caught it' on Anerley Hill. Shop-fronts had disappeared, windows were shattered and broken fragments of glass were everywhere.

The ARP were out in force trying their best to cope with everything.

Our train duly arrived. I wondered if our building where I worked would still be there, as I knew full well that we had really caught a packet that night. I must have dozed off in the train and had therefore not noticed any bomb damage on the journey.

When the train arrived at London Bridge I shot down the tube to the Bank Station and when I came up to the Cornhill exit there was a horrid smell of smoke. Hoses were everywhere, it was very wet and some of the exhausted firemen were being supplied with tea by the WVS and early morning cleaners from the offices.

It was pretty chaotic one way and another. I could see the main buildings still intact, Royal Exchange, Mansion House, Bank of England; though I must admit I was somewhat dazed by it all and shocked as I hurried up Cornhill.

The building where I worked as a telephonist was free from any damage. News travels very fast and by all accounts the wharves around London Bridge were still smouldering. The brave firemen came from all districts in and around London to fight the inferno. So many lost their lives that night. Without their heroism in dealing with the appalling situation, I dread to think what the outcome would have been.

Mr A. Martin was a trained voluntary warden. He also did shift work as a stoker for a block of residential flats in Bloomsbury. He was on the night shift on the night of 29th December:

My first inkling of the extent of the raid was when I noticed that all the water gauges in the boiler houses were dropping fast and I had to sweat like hell to empty the fire-boxes.

The bombing was so heavy that most of the water mains burst and the fires were so fierce that the firemen had to draw water from the Thames.

With one of the house porters I stood on the roof and watched the city burn. It was necessary to be up there because fire bombs were dropping everywhere. It was an awesome sight; away to our right a sea of fire stretched from Trafalgar Square right along to St Paul's. As a stiffening breeze cleared some of the smoke, the dome of the great cathedral was silhouetted against the flames. The swish of water from many hoses could be plainly heard, also the cries of the human beings who were somewhere at work in that inferno.

Now and then there was a surge of bright light upwards to the sky as another missile found its target. Away to our left the university library was in flames and pieces of charred manuscript came drifting on to our roof. When my relief came at 8 a.m. next morning, although I was dog tired, I ventured into the City as far as possible. It was amazing to see the City gents, wearing bowlers and carrying umbrellas and briefcases, trying to get to their offices as though nothing had happened.

John Davey was standing on the porch with his dad and an old neighbour they called 'Mister' and his dog:

Mr Cicanowitz, who was Dutch, was known as 'Mister' simply because we could not pronounce his name. It was a still night when suddenly we heard the drone of a plane which dropped several flares like a giant fireworks display.

The next thing I knew was that everything went grey and I was falling sideways. I eventually settled on my side, trapped by the rubble of our demolished house. I was screaming abuse. My dad's voice came from somewhere near saying, 'Don't worry, son, they will get you out.' 'Mister' just called my dad's name a few times.

After a while I heard voices up above, they heard my shouts and the rescue operations began. From then on I could see the stars in the sky through what appeared to be a small gap.

I could hear the dog trying to find his way out and shouted up to the rescue workers for them to see from where he came out, which they did and this gave them an idea as to where I was. I eventually asked them to lower a torch, which they did and I guided them to me.

The marvellous rescue workers toiled throughout the night and

I was finally rescued after eight hours, but unfortunately my dad, aged 41, and 'Mister' did not survive.

Wyn Wheatcroft recalls taking the train from Epping to London to meet her three brothers who were on their way back from being evacuated:

They didn't turn up for the second time so I made my way back to Liverpool Street Station. I was only fourteen at the time and when I went to the station to get on the train a policeman there asked, 'Where are you going, Missy?' I told him I was going to Epping. 'Not tonight, you're not,' he replied. 'The line has been bombed at Leyton.'

He told me to go to Maryland where a policeman would take me to a shelter. The shelter was over the toilets on an island in the road. It was filled with people, as it was the night they were to bomb London with thousands of incendiary bombs.

There were lots of bus drivers kept coming in saying it was like bonfire night out there. I was being made a fuss of by the bus drivers. They were buying me buns and cups of tea. I don't think I realised how bad it was outside. I remember a WAAF was very kind to me and saw me home the next day as she was stationed at North Weald, so was going my way.

I got a real good hiding when I got home from my mum as she had been worrying about me all night.

Leslie Jerman was eighteen when with his friend, Wally Warren, he drove a Ford Eight to Ludgate Hill in the heart of the City:

We opened the back of the van and poured tea for the firemen. Soon the flames had spread. Incendiaries were added to the fire. We were now in front of St Paul's. All around there were buildings alight. On Ludgate Hill the carpet shop of Treloar's, with its convex glass windows, was ablaze. We emptied our urn and drove back to Plaistow, our base.

Bill Rice was a leading fireman in London and had been called to a house that was completely destroyed. The mother, father and daughter were in an Anderson shelter and had been rescued, but another daughter was in a cot still inside:

Fallen timbers made it impossible to free her from above. Most wardens were fairly hefty fellows and unable to get through the small entrance. One fellow who was slightly built was getting through when I arrived, so I decided to go too and give him assistance. We found that it was impossible to get her from the cot owing to the number of timbers lying across it, and decided she would have to be freed from the bottom. We acquired some cutters and slowly cut away the base and freed her, but our worry was what might shift.

Having with care got her free and with her parents again, I looked for my vehicle and found that it had been directed back to the station. Having got back to Brixton Station I was immediately put on a charge for neglecting my duty and threatened that I might lose my position as a leading fireman. This annoyed me and I told them that I would rather be just a fireman in case something of this nature happened again and after some discussion my explanation was accepted.

E. V. Thompson was a member of the Auxiliary Fire Service on duty in London:

My duty was to drive a Ford V8 with a Denis pump trailer. About ten o'clock that night our crew had a call to report to Stratford Broadway. We immediately started out, driving in the pitch dark, very little light as our headlamps were masked allowing only slits of light. As we neared London, the sky was lit up with flares and the glow of already started fires.

Arriving at the Stratford fire station, we were instructed to proceed to Bromley gas works as various fires were raging there. We were now in the thick of the raid, mines, bombs, incendiaries were falling as if all hell had been let loose. Under those conditions we had little idea as to the route we should take. Another fire crew knew the way and told us to drive close on their tail.

After keeping very close behind we were progressing along the Plaistow Road. Crash, another cascade of incendiaries dropping on the road and houses. With the light from the fires I could plainly see the pump in front.

It was then I had a strange feeling as if a voice was saying, 'Disobey orders and let the leading truck draw away.' As I lifted my foot from the accelerator, dropping behind, I heard shouts. Suddenly I felt as if I was being carried away in a blast of hot sand, increasing noise getting louder and louder until everything blacked out. Quickly regaining consciousness, my immediate thought was of being trapped in a burning vehicle. Crawling out of the car I knelt on the ground. Debris was falling, but my senses told me that although I could not use my steel helmet, it had blown away, I must protect my head. Crawling back to the van I felt for the door opening, lay with my head and shoulders inside until picked up by air-raid wardens who took me to their post and gave me first aid until the ambulance arrived.

Then two wardens came in, most distressed, having to inform the warden attending me that his house had been completely destroyed, there was little hope for his family getting out alive.

A terrible amount of damage had been caused by a parachute mine dropped beside the pump I had been following. The pump's crew completely destroyed, most of the debris had blasted into my car.

The ambulance arrived, being driven by a young woman. On the way to the hospital she stopped to pick up a woman on the road. This woman was swearing like a trooper, vowing that she had only come to the front gate to find out what all the commotion was. A brick must have dropped on her head knocking her unconscious. Partially recovered, bleeding badly, her outcry was her husband indoors would not know where she had gone. Arriving at the hospital to find that it too had been bombed.

Conditions were not good. Water supplies were short. There seemed no room for the wounded. The hospital staff were coping to the best of their ability. Many were kept on the floor in a large hall. During the night the doctors and nurses treated our wounds. I was black from head to foot from the explosive, unable to bath owing to the lack of water. Next morning a car came from Harrow to get me back.

Many, like the parents of Christina Currie, were concerned for the safety of their pets:

My mother and I had two pets. A dog and a cockatoo. They slept in the shelter while the rest of the family went upstairs to their cosy beds in the house.

John Hadley was with the London fire brigade:

Some seconds before the sirens started to wail, we always got the warning by telephone — RED.

During one raid, a scruffy mongrel terrier wandered into our sub-station in Lillie Road School. We adopted him. Needless to say he became known as Red. He remained with us until we were closed by enemy action when he was transferred, with some of the personnel, to the local station at Fulham Road.

He was a bit of a nuisance. When the bells went down for a fire, he would go running along beside the appliances until he was out of breath. He remained at the local station until after the war and was taken on a fire appliance for his final journey.

As Londoners made their way to work in the City on the morning of Monday 30th December, they emerged from the underground and by the light of day looked in horror at what was left of the centre of British commerce. Most of them spent their time attempting to clear the mess from their office buildings. Many found that they had no offices, just a mountain of bricks and smouldering ashes.

The bombing raid lasted 48 hours. In its wake came many problems that demanded solutions. The failure of the water supply meant that the damage inflicted was much greater than it might have been. The firemen who had made a remarkable effort to control the fires deserved better equipment. And the shelters that had seen their share of damage needed assistance. Bank tube station, which so many Londoners had entered for safety, had suffered a direct hit and 111 of the occupants had been killed. If the people of Britain felt there was nowhere they could go for their own safety, it would obviously be just a matter of time before their determination failed.

The raids on London eased up in the New Year, giving the authorities time to deal with the various problems, including new equipment for the fire service. New water mains were laid, designed to be bomb-proof

so that never again would London firemen have to wade through the
Thames in search of water.

Many of those who lived in poor areas and spent every night in the
shelters were near the end of their tether. Thousands gathered in central
London, calling for a 'people's peace'. After heavy raids on Birmingham,
there had been talk of protest there, too.

Ivy Griffiths remembers an attempt to persuade her to join a march
on London:

After night after night of bombings, the planes came over early
without warning, and I was making a mad dash to the shelter at
Grandma's when Mrs Greaves, my next door neighbour, comes
dashing after me, and grabbing my arm said, 'Come with me, I've
had enough and am going to march to London here and now
and put an end to the bombing.' Suddenly there was an almighty
bang. She turned tail and ran and I made for the shelter as fast as
I could. That was the end of any further suggestions of a march
to London.

Dreadful weather forced the Luftwaffe to stay where they were for
a month, giving the population of London a period of quiet. The
government were able to tackle the problems that had forced so many
into the streets in protest. Thousands of bunk beds appeared in the
large shelters, helping to smother the growing discontent.

11

The Last of the Raids

Bristol, Cardiff, Portsmouth and many of the smaller centres were soon back on the bombing list. Those fighting the war at sea had no guarantee that their port of arrival would be a haven. Signalman Eric Willee was on a destroyer which put into Portsmouth on the day following an air-raid:

The off-duty members of the crew were split into pairs, each pair was provided with a stirrup-pump, a bucket and small axe and sent ashore as fire-fighting parties to deal with the second night of air-raid fires.

I was paired with Wireless Telegraphist Peter Webster; we were sent to Kings Road, Southsea. When we arrived, the Kings Road seemed to be ablaze from end to end. As we walked along the road a policeman dismounted from his bicycle, 'Are you a fire-fighting party?' 'Yes!' 'Then get on with it!'

I explained that with our modest equipment we needed to find a small fire. He rode off in disgust. The only noise was of fire and partial collapse of houses. The people were in shelters and there were no exploding bombs. All the damage that night was caused by incendiary bombs as far as we could see.

We spotted a house with smoke coming from the eaves. After a lot of banging on the door a very pale lady answered and said that her husband was out seeing a patient and that we must find another doctor. We persuaded her to come to the pavement to see the smoke coming from her house. She reluctantly allowed us into the house. (Young sailors were not highly regarded by the intelligentsia until the loss of HMS *Hood*.)

Peter filled the bath with cold water and I climbed into the roof space. It was filthy and full of smoke, a faint glow was visible at a point where the roof met the wall and there was a clean hole in the roof just over my head. The doctor's wife passed the nozzle of the pump to me, Peter started pumping and I was able to direct a small stream of water at the bomb.

In a short while the glow disappeared, steam mingled with the smoke and I called to Peter to stop pumping and started to lower myself through the hatch. About three rungs down the ladder both my legs were firmly grasped. Our policeman friend had decided to take charge. 'Get back up there and finish the job,' he said. 'It is finished and I'm coming down,' I said. The doctor's wife was repeatedly asking, 'What's going on?' and Peter was telling the policeman to let me go.

As soon as I reached the floor the policeman grabbed the hose end and ascended the ladder to finish the job. He was a big man and quite unable to get through the hatch. He ordered me to get into the roof and follow his instructions. I refused to do so. Peter was equally unco-operative, so he placed us under arrest.

We were taken to Portsmouth police station, questioned and put in a cell. Peter was telling me his opinion (worth listening to since he was a solicitor in civilian life) about whether we would be safer in prison than on the high seas, when he heard the familiar voice of our captain demanding our immediate release and addressing the sort of remarks we would like to have made to our custodians.

Lillian Kerslake (now Smith) was nine when the war started and was living on the outskirts of Plymouth when the city was bombed on in March, 1941. Her mother had taken her to the city for a church service which concluded at 8 p.m.:

We could not leave the building as there was a lot of bombing and the streets were ablaze with fires. After a while a bomb was dropped near where we were and the building came in on us. My mother took me by the hand and pulled me out of the rubble and we ran down the road looking for an air-raid shelter. Eventually an air-raid warden told us to go into the Charles Street churchyard shelter which I can remember was very crowded and dark.

In that shelter I heard people saying that a bomb had been dropped very near to us and the blast was felt round our legs and had this blast passed higher we would have died because our lungs would have collapsed.

Dorothy Marshall and her husband were in the middle of Plymouth when the bombs began to fall. Her husband asked her to wait as he dashed off to see if he could help:

There was a lovely smell of roast pork coming from the shop on whose window-sill I was sitting. It was minutes before I realised that the shop was a delicatessen and it was blazing behind me.

Ten-year-old Billy Clark was with his family during the bombing of Plymouth:

The time was 7.35 in the evening. Mother tells me to turn on the radio as there was a programme she wanted to listen to that started at 8 p.m. From the radio came the terrible noise of static, nothing of the programme could be heard. 'Turn it off,' says Mum, 'we will try again later.'

At 8 o'clock she turned it on again. This time a man's voice is screaming, 'Take cover, take cover! There are hundreds of them.' A few seconds later the sirens started wailing. Mother says to Aunt Jessie, 'Take Billy and Cynthia to the shelter. I will get Jean and follow on.' Jean is in bed asleep.

We put on our overcoats (we always put on overcoats when going to the shelter whatever the weather) and Cynthia was first out of the door, followed by me and Aunt Jessie carrying the bags of extra bits and pieces to take to the shelter, cushions, blankets, and a hot drink if there was time to make one.

We run to the shelter, which is about 200 yards away in another street. We have been trained to keep close to the walls of the buildings in the street and to pause in doorways every twenty yards or so to let the grown-ups catch up.

We reached the shelter, at least they called it a shelter, it was actually the basement of a three or four-storeyed warehouse which had been reinforced with brick internal walls. The air-raid warden recognised us as regulars and said, 'Come on in, son. You know the way.'

I woke suddenly to noise and confusion. I felt heavy pressure all over me. We had been bombed and were now buried. I tried to force myself through the rubble but I didn't have the strength.

The only thing I could do was move my right forefinger. I don't know how long we were buried because I drifted in and out of consciousness. Eventually I awoke to find that my legs were cold. I had been partially uncovered by the rescue workers. I had the sense to move my legs from side to side to attract attention to myself. I felt a hand on my knee and heard a man's comforting voice saying, 'All right, son. We know you are there.' A few minutes later the rescuers finished digging me out and carried me to an ambulance. I remember being surprised at finding that the ambulance driver was a young woman. I thought only men could drive.

There were no doors on the back of the ambulance. I was on one of four stretchers strapped in for safety. As we drove through the streets of Plymouth, I could see that the whole sky was lit up by the fires on the ground. We were driven through burning streets and frequently bumped over bits of rubble. Our young driver found her way through all the damage and confusion to the hospital. The last thing I remembered was a man with a bald head bending over me saying, 'Hello, son. What's wrong with you?'

While my rescue was taking place, Mum and Cynthia had been taken to another shelter a few yards from the one we were in.

Some time later there was a lull in the bombing, Mum and Cynthia made their way out of the shelter to go home for a cup of tea. As she got to the door an officious air-raid warden said, 'You can't go back in there yet. The all clear hasn't gone.' Mum, who was only about five foot three inches tall, grabbed hold of the front of the man's uniform and said, 'Listen you! I have just had my sister killed in that shelter over the road, my five-year-old daughter went as well and I don't even know where my son is.' Still shaking the man by his coat she continued, 'I am going in my home for a cup of tea and you and nobody else is going to stop me.'

(I was told later that Aunt Jessie had been killed outright by the bomb and my sister had been alive for a while but the dust in the rubble covered her head and she suffocated.)

Of the 22 persons in the shelter, eleven died, three of them babies in prams.

Nine of the family of Ursula Paula Beaven (now Bullen) were killed in the Plymouth blitz in March, 1941:

The bombing had gone on for five nights with the warning siren sounding at 7.25 p.m. to the minute every night — that in itself was infuriating.

After school on the fateful day, I was then aged fifteen years, I accompanied my great-aunt to take tea at the home of my mother's eldest brother, William, as her younger brother Francis had sustained a broken leg in a public house which had been bombed the previous evening. I promised to join my Uncle Frank and travel to the hospital in a taxi the following morning. We left the house about 6.45 p.m. in order to reach home by the prescribed time for the air-raids.

The next day I set out to keep my morning appointment and on the way met another of my mother's brothers, Uncle Bart, his wife, eighteen-month-old twin sons and five-year-old daughter at an in-law's house. Everyone threw their arms around me and cried. After a period of time I realised they were telling me their house had been burned down by incendiary bombs and they had escaped and at the tail end of the raid had walked through the devastation to William's house only to find it in ruins after a direct hit.

At the behest of Uncle Bart I went down to William's house to tell the men who were digging out exactly who was in the house at tea-time the previous day.

When I reached my destination I saw my cousin Sheila's fur coat hanging over the telegraph wires across the street. This coat was later returned to the family. Winding my way through a small group of people I was recognised by one of the men digging in the ruins. He knew my mother and her brothers. I noted only one part-wall was standing, on which was a shelf holding a glass bowl which contained eggs, some unbroken.

I gave the men the required information and left. On looking over my shoulder some moments later I saw the rescue man still standing on the same spot as if rooted. The tears were pouring down his begrimed face.

Joan Gates (now Stone) had been transferred to the air-raid casualty department in the Southern Hospital in Dartford, Kent:

A stretcher case arrived with his head bandaged. I asked the ambulance man if it was a head case. The casualty promptly sat up and said, 'Far from it, nurse.' He thought I had said 'dead'!

One night, I recall, when the raids were heavy, I was on the men's ward — I was as frightened as anybody, but of course could never show fear — I used to sit by the bedside of little boys who were in bed and hold their hands. To help both of us!

Marjorie Ulph was sitting in a concrete shelter in the back yard of her Hull home when the bombs started to drop.

We heard them whistling down and we used to say, 'This one isn't for us as we can hear it whistling.' When it did hit the ground the earth would rock.

When we came out of the shelter, we saw all the damage, all the windows broken and a big gap at the corner of the street where seven people lost their lives.

My aunt, who lived at Dennington, near Sheffield, saw a huge red glow in the sky and was told that it was Hull on fire. My aunt took a train to Hull and walked through the wreckage of our house (no buses). When she took one look at my mother and burn into tears saying, 'I never thought I'd see you alive again.'

Muriel Keymer came from East Anglia but was living with her husband, Alfred, in Rugby. One night she woke with a start and asked her husband if they would go home if anything happened to her parents. He assured her that they would, and both went back to sleep.

I went to sleep only in the morning to hear that a town in East Anglia had been bombed. I knew. It was not until the Wednesday that the telegram arrived. '48 demolished. No trace.'

It seemed incredible that this could happen to me. We went immediately and found the train full with forces going home on compassionate leave. The naval people found me a seat and a cup of tea. A petty officer asked me where I was bound for and I showed him the telegram.

Arriving at Norwich we met my brother. He was in the army and together we walked to my sister's home, quite a distance. The searchlights were up and we knew another raid was imminent. They came as we got to my sister's house and the six of us crouched under a Morrison shelter. The bombing started, the ground shook and I prayed to die. The raid seemed to last for hours and we eventually, with the help of an air-raid warden, dragged ourselves out.

Outside were men from all over the country, their fire hoses trailing in the streets. All my sister's windows were blown out and filled with brown material whilst tanks called around with fresh water, which had to be boiled.

As soon as possible we went to see if our parents, sister and niece had been found and when I saw my old home flattened and rescue workers digging the rubble I was too tired to cry. They asked me if I knew what the kitchen covering was like and as I stood there I wondered why it had to be them.

Finally I went to the City Hall to see the town clerk to ascertain what teams had been at work there. Despite much opposition, I succeeded in finding the assistant town clerk, who knew me and eventually I found that the bodies of my parents, or rather my mother, had been found. Alfred eventually found my baby niece and her neck had been broken. My sister he identified by her hands. My mother was in a bag labelled 'Elderly lady with hair going grey.' My father they never found. Although the roofs were searched for weeks after, they eventually buried an arm.

The bombing of London was far from over. On 19th March the Luftwaffe were back again in even bigger numbers. They left behind 750 dead civilians.
Elsie Noades lived over some shops in Hampstead:

The premises received a direct hit. My son and I were buried for twenty hours. From 1 p.m. Friday to 9 a.m. Saturday. He was three and half years old at the time. I remember coming to and feeling him by my side, impressing on him to keep his eyes shut. Consequently he was blind for four days. The debris had got into his eyes. My legs were trapped and I had a nail in my forehead which I managed to wriggle out. Anyway, if it had not been for my mum and dad, I'd have been there now. Fire broke out and there was a gas explosion. The warden said no-one could survive under these conditions. My parents insisted that I must be there, because normally I would light a fire for them and do a little shopping and had I gone anywhere I would have left a note. The next morning a hundred men were put on the site and began digging. I was found at 9 a.m. My first words were, 'What is the time?'

Everybody cheered as I was brought out. My mother on hearing that I had been found and that my legs were trapped said: 'Cut them off. Get her out.'

Pam Rendell (now Wood) was three and suffering from a bone disease. She was unable to walk and had been transferred to the Queen Elizabeth Hospital for Sick Children in Carshalton, Surrey:

The particular night in question I absolutely refused to eat my bread and milk supper, even when they added cocoa, and as a punishment I was taken out of the main ward and out in a side ward on my own, in complete darkness. Some time later the air-raid warning sounded and as usual, all the children were carried down to the air-raid shelter.

Unfortunately, as there had been a shift change of the nursing staff, I was forgotten and nobody came for me. I was unable to move as I was in a plaster cast and by the time that I realised what was happening, nobody could hear my cries.

That was the most terrifying night of my life. When I close my eyes I can still see the explosions of light and darkness, the whining sound as they fell through the air, followed by the unmistakable 'thrump' when the bombs hit the ground and then the ear-splitting sound of the explosions.

I hid under the blankets with my eyes shut tight and my hands over my ears, but could not blot out either the flames or the noise.

I felt sure that the hospital had been hit and because I had been naughty I had gone straight to hell.

In spite of the air-raids some aspects of life went along much as they always had. The future Mrs Lynton was six and her sister nine when they found, much to their sorrow, that school had changed very little:

One day we were sent back from school because a land mine had landed in the grounds but had not exploded. We were disappointed when it was disarmed safely — we had thought we had the chance of a holiday if the school blew up.

If the siren went during school hours we would go to the shelters and continue our lessons there, though they were usually in the form of spelling bees, mental arithmetic, quizzes and sing-songs. If the all clear had not gone by the end of the morning or afternoon school, we were not allowed to go home unless an adult had come to collect us.

My mother would collect us, putting up her umbrella to keep off any falling shrapnel etc, and we would all march home quite confident of its ability to protect us.

The children would go shrapnel-gathering in the morning. Bits of shrapnel were popular collectors' pieces and were swopped for comics, small toys etc. Everybody hoped to find the tail-fins of incendiary bombs which were reputed to be of fabulous value. I never saw any tail-fins and to be honest am not sure that they existed, or alternatively that they survived the fire that the bomb caused.

The teenaged daughter of a neighbour was in their garden when an incendiary bomb landed near her but did not ignite on landing. She tried to disable it by putting a dustbin lid on top but this made it explode causing a lot of damage. She was reported in the *Daily Mirror* because of this. We all thought she was stupid — we knew that you were supposed to put earth or sand on an incendiary bomb, and all I could think of was that it was a waste of a good tail-fin

Jean Hewitt (now Emmins) was thirteen and had returned to London after being evacuated:

Father was in a reserved occupation at Tooting and Mum was called to a munitions factory at Earlsfield. Even though we never knew if we'd be together again in the evening we all went about our affairs in a relatively light-hearted manner, never hugging or kissing each other goodbye. It was surprising how life went on in spite of the war. I went to the cinema regularly and most Saturday nights I went dancing to the Streatham Locarno.

June Smith (now Harmer) was seven when war broke out. She and her sister had also been evacuated but returned to their parents' home in London:

Each night we went to the public shelter where we slept in three-tier bunk beds. There was row upon row of them in the basement of the furniture shop. Dad slept in the top bunk, my sister in the bottom one and Mum and I in the middle. We would go to the shelter as soon as we had eaten our tea and Dad would join us when he got home. Some nights he didn't come home, as he was in his company's fire brigade and was often on night duty.

During breaks in the raids we would go across the road to a cafe by the Hackney Empire to get a jug of tea. If the siren went while you were queuing up, you had to decide whether to give up your place in the queue and take shelter or take a chance and get your tea.

The future Pauline Scowen was eleven in 1940. She was evacuated, but later returned to London and remained there for the rest of the war:

We lived in Wandsworth on an estate and some of the ground floor flats were made into air-raid shelters by means of iron poles being fitted to strengthen them. However, when the top block of flats was hit one night (we lived on a hill and the block we lived in was at the bottom), all the people in the shelters were crushed because the iron poles buckled.

They changed these to wooden beams after that, but my mother had lost faith in the shelters then, so we stayed in our own flat. I remember her saying, 'If we go, we all go together.'

I remember at school being told to be very quiet in the play-ground because the fire-fighters had been fighting fires all night and were trying to sleep. We stood around in little groups whispering and sometimes watching the dog-fights high in the sky and the boys always knew which were ours.

The railway line ran at the back of us and at night, a train fitted with what was called a 'pom-pom gun' would go past firing at the bombers lit up by the searchlights.

When I started work, I worked at Ross Optical works at Clapham Common and often women — for it was mostly women doing the war work — would not come to work one morning and we would later hear that their house had been bombed that night and we would not see them again. There would then be a collection for a wreath.

Many of the children were quick to recognise the different planes. Although only twelve, James Giles considered himself an expert:

My friend Peter was eleven. We stood chatting outside my home when an aeroplane appeared overhead. 'Wow, that's a German Junkers 90,' I said. 'No,' said Peter, 'there's no air-raid on — it's an RAF Blenheim.' 'Bet you it's a Junkers,' I replied. Suddenly we saw clearly a bomb descending from its underbelly. We shot into the house; a loud explosion followed. 'Told you so!' I uttered.

Helen Walton saw a parachute descending near her home in south London, and set off with others determined to catch the enemy airman:

You can appreciate that this could not be in a straight line, but up roads, round corners, etc, but always keeping 'him' in sight. Then someone realised we were chasing not a human, but a land mine gently swinging from the skies. You can imagine the immediate turn around as it was pretty low and this time garden fences and any other obstacle was taken in our stride.

One way of finding out what people valued most was seeing them attempting to retrieve their valuables from their bombed houses. Fireman Tini Wright hurried to help a woman outside the ruin of her house in London:

She saw her house had been destroyed and remarked, 'Oh, well, I still have my bloody pawn ticket.'

Jean Shakespeare (now Rush) had a bomb drop in her back yard several miles from central London:

When the bomb dropped the house shook, but amazingly no windows were broken, although the black-out was blown down. I can remember running over the whole house turning off lights and was quite a heroine for a few days. Everyone else was too petrified to think about the black-out, but I suppose at the age of ten I wasn't aware of what a close shave we had had.

I remember my father and uncle (who was in the Home Guard) went out into the garden to see what had fallen. My father came back saying, 'There's a hell of a hole out there!' which was a family joke for the rest of his life as the understatement of the year. Luckily we had a long garden and my mother had made an allotment at the end of it. The ground was well dug and wet, so the bomb, a fifty-pounder, had buried deep before exploding.

The main thing I remember next day when we went out and saw the crater in the daylight, there were cabbages stuck in the row of poplar trees at the end of the garden.

Irene Martin recalls living on the fringes of the City of London:

When the blitz started we went to a local shelter but this became too crowded and uncomfortable. Someone mentioned to my mother that there was a better shelter situated in Clerkenwell

Road, which was known as Foresters Hall. It was quite a deep shelter and consisted of bays each of which had a few wooden contraptions which you could make up as beds and also a few three-tier bunks. The shelter itself was a mass of grey concrete and always felt damp and cold.

The trek to the shelter started as soon as it got dark or when the wireless ceased broadcasting. We had bundles of bedding and odds and ends and, like refugees, would make our way. After making up our beds we would sit and talk. Lots of women took up knitting and we would make friends with families in the other bays. There were always one or two wardens about on top to keep an eye open for any incendiary bombs and, in general, look after us.

Once the dreaded siren had sounded we tried to be normal, hoping for the best, I suppose. Eventually everyone would try to get some sleep and, being young, I suppose it was a lot easier for me. Of course, we all slept in our clothes, which was horrible. You could hear the noise going on in a muffled sort of way.

Early in the morning everyone would pack up their belongings and head for home and the thing that stays with me is seeing miles and miles (or so it seems) of firemen's hoses lying all along the roads and the smell of burning. Once home I used to crawl into bed for some extra sleep until it was time to get ready for school.

Whilst Mum, my two sisters and myself went to the shelter, my father insisted on staying home to look after things, although he used to check up on neighbours who refused to leave their homes.

After a while the bombing became very intense and very frightening and in the middle of one particular night, after the all clear had sounded, our wardens insisted we get up to look at the sight outside. We could hardly believe our eyes as the whole of the City seemed to be on fire and even the factory next to our shelter, which I believe was owned by May and Baker, the chemists, was burning. You can imagine how lucky we were to be so close to everything and still be safe. We really believed that the square mile of the City had gone forever.

Eventually, after so many weeks of the same routine, my mum

had had enough and I will never forget it was a Saturday night, my sisters had already gone to the shelter and my dad was creating merry hell because my mum refused to go. Well, on time as usual, the wireless went quiet, the siren sounded and over they came. The bombs started to fall and the ack-ack guns created such horrendous noise that Mum soon realised how silly she had been, so we made for the local shelter, running all the way, and we could hear the shrapnel falling about us and we were terrified. Obviously we made it all right and the experience was never repeated.

I must tell you that apart from all the terrible things that were happening, the atmosphere at Foresters Hall was fantastic; everyone was friendly and helped others less fortunate, there were many laughs listening to the elderly tell stories of the past etc. Certain things come to mind such as the night the rumour went round that a parachute had been found on top and we thought the invasion had started, and someone mentioned that a man was sitting on his own in one of the bays whom nobody had ever seen before and we wondered if he was a spy. On tackling him, one of the wardens found out that the poor man had been caught out in the raid and had come into the shelter for safety. Incidentally the parachute was a piece of a barrage balloon that had come down.

Another incident concerned Dad when, during a very heavy raid, he tried to get an elderly spinster in our street down the shelter whereupon she said she couldn't leave without her cat. The short answer from Dad was, 'Sod the cat!'

Rose Headeck and her husband were living in Carshalton, Surrey. They had a young daughter and son:

The small bedroom was downstairs with a triangle window. My husband sand-bagged the window up and put our table tennis top over the lot and fixed it to the wall. We had a mattress on the floor to sleep on. My husband's mother, who lived in Ramsgate, wrote to us and asked if she could come up and stay with us, which she did. The siren went off, my mother-in-law was sleeping on the camp-bed and our son in his cot in the lounge. We all went into the small room and stayed there until the all-clear siren went off. Mother said she would go back to bed. I was a little uneasy walking up and down the hall with Allan in my arms.

As things seemed to have quietened down, Mother went to bed and I put Allan back in his cot. My husband, daughter and I went back to lie on the mattress in the refuge room. We had hardly been there a few minutes when I saw a silver light go down the boarded window. I came round later in hospital.

When my husband came to see me he told me we had lost our home. His dear mother had been killed and our son, being so small, had gone through the house and was found outside the dining room window. He had been taken to another hospital.

I was told afterwards that the plane had dropped four 500-pound bombs. The crater in our front garden and part of our home you could put two double decker buses in. The council found us a house to live in until our first one was rebuilt in 1947.

The King and Queen divided their time between London and the relative safety of Windsor. They frequently made trips to bombed areas to give the residents encouragement. Sarah Cartwright had gone to the theatre in the West End to celebrate her mother's 75th birthday:

Nearing the end of the performance, the siren went and they announced that the show would go on, but advised people in the balcony to come downstairs and they would entertain us all until the all clear sounded, otherwise they could go to the local shelter.

We decided to stay and enjoy the sing-song that followed, but when things seemed to quiet down outside we thought we would make for the underground and wend our way home to Kennington. We had just started our trek to the tube when the barrage started up again, so we hurried down the air-raid shelter in Piccadilly.

We hadn't been there very long before three men in tin hats and uniforms came running down the steps, and one of them was the King! He came around and spoke to us all and complimented my mother on her courage at venturing out and when she told him it was her birthday he wished her many happy returns.

After a while the bombs were still raining down and the air-raid warden who accompanied the King said he had to leave as he would be needed. The King said, 'Just a minute and I'll be with you,' but the warden said, 'But Sir, it's too dangerous for you. I'm going because it's my job.' The King replied, 'It is my job too!'

Different people had different fears. Pam Gibbons (now Buckland) lived in Balham:

Mum's personal fear was that the house would fall about her ears as she sat on the 'lav' or took a bath and these essential operations were carried out at high speed. I was more afraid that I might see a dead person, or worse, half a dead person, after a neighbour related the grisly story of seeing the lower part of a man standing at his garden gate — no one asked where the rest of him was.

John Barber was eleven and living in Hackney Marshes. The marsh was used as a dumping ground for much of the debris resulting from the bombing and was a perfect place to explore for discarded 'treasures':

When Reeves and Sons, the famous artists' materials suppliers, was bombed we found a wonderful selection of paint, watercolours and inks all in very good condition. We had to move very carefully just to salvage it, as the lorries continued tipping and at times it could be dangerous. These materials were a prize for me and my pal, Wally.

Hester Stephens (now Wood) was living in Sunbury-on-Thames. She had arrived at the railway station to catch the train to school only to find that it had received a direct hit in the night:

The immediate reaction of my fellow passengers and myself was of rejoicing that we wouldn't be able to get to school — only to find that the Southern Railway had set up a bus shuttle to the next station, Hampton, where we could easily walk to school.

The City gents with their bowler hats and pin-striped trousers and inevitable rolled-up umbrellas claimed all the seats and we girls, clad in our nunlike grey wool, clutching lunches and grey gym knickers, swayed in the aisle.

At Hampton, everyone filed off the bus. We girls gathered in a little group deciding what was to be done to delay facing incarceration as long as possible, when a gentleman, impeccably dressed for town, caught our attention. He suddenly started searching his pockets, at first calmly, then in desperation, looking for his handkerchief, which he failed to find. Then he let out an ear-splitting, uncontrolled sneeze. But oh, horror. With the sneeze a complete set of dentures flew through the air as if jet-propelled and landed in the gutter.

The bus driver decided to back his bus out of the station yard and the poor City gent stood paralysed with horror as the bus ran over his dentures and then forward again to adjust for a better turn. He gave a little cry of despair and did a feeble little leap in the air, then disappeared into the gents' cloakroom.

Many people were bombed out more than once. Marion Eason's mother lost three homes and each time she walked about the streets with an old wheelbarrow or pram, salvaging what she could:

I was born in 1941, February of that year. In the same year we lost our first home in an air-raid and I caught diphtheria at ten months of age.

Dad was serving in the Royal Navy, fighting abroad most of the time. Mum, being a true Cockney, was one of fourteen children. Poverty was a natural part of life for her and her family. But their poverty-stricken lives helped them survive.

Mum said she used to get a really bad feeling just before she was bombed out, like a premonition I suppose. The first time I was only a baby and Mum had this awful feeling that something was going to happen. She got me all ready, sat me in the pram while she got her bits and pieces together. She left the pram at the house and carried me across London to visit her brother.

There was no transport running and as she walked there was an air-raid. She must have found shelter somewhere.

The next day my dad came home on leave. He went to the house and found it as flat as a pancake.

Edith Dowse was bombed out four times. The first time was at Queen's Road, Wimbledon:

We backed on to the railway line — it was used for pom-pom guns going up and down during the raids. The Town Hall at the bottom of the road was used as an air-raid shelter. During the many daytime raids and alerts this was quite a meeting place for local mums with children to congregate. We grabbed our babies and our knitting and dashed for the shelter.

I was rushing past the Town Hall with my son in his pram one day when the warden shouted to me to take cover. I had only a hundred yards to go and wanted to get home. He dragged me and the pram under cover just in time, because when I got home the baby's nappies looked like a colander with bullet holes.

Our next move took us to West Hill, Wandsworth. Our flat was in a large house next to the art college. Soldiers had been billeted but had now vacated the premises, but they forgot to tell Hitler. Dozens of bombs rained down one night and more were dropped at the top of the hill where a great number of Americans were housed.

We were got out, given a cup of tea and sat on the pavement — a pitch-dark night lit up like day with fires and buildings in flames. Once again we were rehoused but left some of our good furniture in storage. A rosewood piano was left for three years and when we retrieved it and unlocked it we found that the inside was missing, presumably blown out, just leaving the outer casing.

It was difficult enough for those who were healthy. Margaret Townsend's grandmother had the added problem of being in a wheelchair:

Because of this she always insisted that when there was an air-raid she would stay under the stairs of the house, as it was too much for my mother to lift both her and the chair down to the shelter. Mum, having settled my grandmother, took me with her down to the shelter in the garden.

Some time later a bomb exploded at the side of the house. As Mum and I came out of the shelter it was like being in a thick fog. I can remember hearing my mother scream, 'Are you safe, Mum?' When the dust started to clear my grandmother was in her chair, calling back that she was all right. A small part of the wall beside her was intact and hanging from it was a glass-framed picture of myself which had not been damaged at all.

My mother, who was completely shocked by this experience, said to me, 'I'll find somewhere for the two of us to have a drink.' She had never been to a public house before on her own but in the two of us went. We sat with our drinks in our hands, our faces as black as coal. We must have looked a strange sight.

Paul Wilks was eating breakfast with his mother and sister when the sirens sounded in Swindon, Wiltshire. They immediately crawled into their Morrison shelter with the breakfast and continued eating. The local infants' school was well prepared for air-raids and had regular practices:

Mrs Williams, the headmistress, would tell us that she was going to ring the bell and when we heard it we were to make our way to the shelter. The real thing occurred one afternoon during classes. Our teacher, Miss Hitchin, told us to follow her to the shelter. I remember thinking at the time, 'Why didn't silly old Miss Williams tell us she was going to ring the bell, as she had done in the past?'

With her younger sister Patricia, who was two and a half, eight-year-old Maureen Jones (now Renshaw) lived close to the Fairey aircraft factory in Manchester, a regular target for the bombers. There was a public shelter close by:

As the sirens sounded, my aunt and mum used to put the youngest children in their prams — one at each end — place the old tin baths over the tops and run like hell across to the shelter.

Doris Roberts (now Monk)'s married sister and her husband owned a butcher's shop in Edmonton, north London:

The bombing had been very bad there for several weeks. My sister kept saying, 'Oh, for a good night's sleep, properly, in your pyjamas.' They had an opportunity to spend the weekend in the country away from it all, in a caravan at Waltham Cross (only a few miles from Edmonton).

They duly went. The first night a bomb fell in the same field as the caravan, blew them completely out of bed, out of the caravan into the field, complete in their pyjamas — and to top it all, my sister was more scared of the cows than the bombs!

John Norris's father, Charlie, was the local ARP watchkeeper/ambulance driver. Although they were living in the country, they had experienced bombing from attacks on nearby Swansea:

An alert was called, there was an air-raid imminent, so Dad sounded the siren. He became concerned as to how my mother would cope with me and my elderly grandmother who lived with us. In a state of rising anxiety, he ran through the darkened streets to our house. As he had feared, my mother was in a state of some agitation trying to dress a squalling child, trying to persuade Gran to come to the shelter, while at the same time getting together blankets and a little food to take to the shelter in case the alert was long drawn-out as they often were.

Gran settled her side of the argument by locking herself in the stair cupboard with her savings and pension books: a few precious possessions and Dad's shop takings for the week stowed inside a large copper kettle.

Hurriedly my mother and father gathered what was needed into a bundle and Mother set off down the street leaving this, while my father, having strapped me into my folding wheelchair, set off pushing me in this after her.

It was dark. So dark that Dad ran me at full tilt into a lamp-post. He went sprawling and my carriage and I spun off into the pitch black night. Desperation. Time was running out and he could hear the drone of aero engines approaching. How did he find me? '*Bawl!*' Father used to say. 'I'd have heard him above the sound of my siren.' There I was. Upside down in the middle of the street strapped in the wheelchair and bawling like a bull. Dad gathered me up and ran with me still upside down in the pushchair to the Town Hall and practically hurled me down the steps into the dimly lit basement among the folk who had already settled there.

My parents were resigned to the possibility that Gran had 'copped it'. Why, oh why didn't the stubborn old thing come to the refuge with us? At first light came the 'all clear'. Father had to go off to sound it, while Mum and I set off to see what was left of our home. It was still there, minus its windows and sundry slates and fittings, but substantially intact.

Gran? . . . Gran was curled up on a rug in the stair cupboard sound asleep. She woke up with the steely dignity she always possessed and made us a cup of tea, but only after restoring the valuable items she had clutched through the night to their rightful places.

The raids continued throughout Britain and in April, 1941, Coventry was once again chosen as the target. Doreen Robbins, who was ten, had taken cover under the stairs with her two older brothers:

My mother was puttering about in the kitchen as she always did. My father had built a little bed underneath the stairs. We always went under there when the bombing was on, though we had an Anderson shelter in the garden and a Morrison shelter we didn't use either. The dog used the Morrison as a kennel and we never went out into the Anderson because it was always full of water. Then we heard this big one coming and my mother dived under the stairs with us. The house was demolished. It took the wardens and firemen about half an hour to get us out, including the dog. A fireman carried me out over his shoulder through the bombing and the dog followed. He ran through the streets and left me in another shelter all by myself. My uncle, who was also a fireman, found me and took me back to my parents. My father, who was working for the railroad at the time, came back and found the house demolished and of course, thought we were all gone. So he was just sat outside on the pavement crying.

Although Eire was neutral during the war, Northern Ireland was involved and making just as many sacrifices as anyone else.

In April Belfast received a terrible pounding. During the raid, fire engines from their southern neighbour raced across the border between the two countries to help.

The night raids continued through the spring and climaxed in a shocking raid on London on 10th May. With the raid expanded to cover a much larger area, the casualties reached record numbers. Some of Britain's most majestic buildings, the House of Commons, Westminster Abbey, the Tower of London, the Law Courts and the Royal Mint, were hit and badly damaged.

Pearl Sutton (now Le Serve) was working in an amusement arcade in Tottenham Court Road when it received a direct hit:

I was buried forty feet I am told. It apparently was on the placards next morning. Everyone was killed. The manager, his son and several staff including my husband who I had only been married to for seven months. So I was engaged, married and a widow at 21. I understand it was a wall that saved me. I was in a sort of alcove. I remember being asked what religion I was while still being buried — having been thrown on my stomach, I was just able to talk and move my fingers slightly.

I was telling someone I felt they were walking over me — however I was asked if I knew what direction I was. I can remember being dug out and there was great difficulty getting my feet out, consequently I've had bother ever since and I now wear a leg iron.

Pearl Sunshine lived with her husband and parents in a large Edwardian house between Regent's Park and Mornington Crescent. She was in her twenties and had been married a year. Her husband was in uniform, but stationed in London. She remembered one of the last big raids on the capital:

I had great faith in our solid old house and was determined to stay in it at night whenever the sirens sounded. So my husband had brought our bed down to the basement and there we slept. On that particular night my husband, with some sixth sense of premonition, advised me to sleep in my clothes and not to undress, as he thought it was going to be a bad night. I took his advice and still remember the clothes I wore to go to bed in that night — a yellow roll-neck sweater and beige corduroy trousers. My parents had departed to Liberty's shelter and my husband and I went to bed as usual.

I don't know exactly what time it was but I think it was late, perhaps eleven or twelve o'clock, when we heard this enormous explosion and the windows were blown into the room and the black-out curtains hurled across the other side. I thought the shock had made me cry and that there were tears rolling down my cheeks, but it was actually scores of tiny fragments of glass that had embedded themselves to my face, eyelids, ears and hair, and it was blood that was trickling down my face.

At the same time we heard horrendous bangs taking place within the house. Everything from the top of the house had fallen to the bottom and we were literally entombed in our basement room.

Even fully dressed I was shivering, but my husband was absolutely wonderful. He found my shoes and coat and his own shoes and taking me by the hand, hauled me up the ever-descending pile of furniture, bricks and rubble to a little space that he could see had not been filled. We made it to the ground floor and what was left of the front of the house.

Although the middle of the night, it was as light as day from the fires raging in the vicinity of Tottenham Court Road and even nearer.

A passing taxi stopped and the driver called out, 'You look in a bad way, Miss, get in the taxi — I'm taking this young lady and baby to the hospital.' My husband and I got into the taxi. The young woman was in her nightdress and the driver took us to the Temperance Hospital in Hampstead Road. I was placed on a stretcher and the pieces of glass extracted from my face with tweezers. I remember distinctly lots of pieces of glass falling out of my long hair which dangled over the edge of the stretcher as I was being carried into the hospital. My face was painted — I looked in the mirror later and thought I looked like a Red Indian. My husband had disappeared and I found out later that he had gone on to the roof of the hospital and was helping to put out fire bombs.

The final tally was almost 1500 killed, the largest number in one night of any raid. Thousands were without gas or water.

It was the last major air-raid on London. Despite the devastation, the blitz was over.

Postscript

Although the war was far from being won, and the V1 and V2 bombers which terrorised London in the later years were yet to come, the British people would never again have to endure the persistent and exhausting onslaught of 1940–1941.

A number of the survivors remember the camaraderie that seemed to survive anything Hitler could throw at it. Millie Driscoll writes:

People trusted each other. Our homes were very insecure, one push and our front door was open — quite often it would be wide open when we came home from the tube, but there were no robberies that I heard about, certainly nothing was taken from our house. People were glad to be alive and not envious of each other, except perhaps in the food queues if they thought someone got more than they should.

Recently the media have been reporting that we were a healthier nation during the war because of a much better diet. I sometimes think exercise and fear had something to do with it — when the warning went, fear gave us almost the speed of the best athlete to get to the shelter, and before the tube was declared an official shelter we were not allowed to use the lift. We had to go down the emergency stairs and come back up them. I can't remember how many there were, but I think it was well over 150, so you didn't have much chance to get fat.

Marion Eason's family had been poor even before war broke out:

Our poverty didn't end with the war, it took a good many years to recover. But we still kept laughing and eating our porridge!

Edna Beeson's memories are less rosy:

We were robbed of six years of our lives. The rationing, the black-out, the fire-watching of our places of work (many must have been killed whilst guarding the premises of absent landlords), and the deaths of friends and former colleagues in the forces are all contrary to the idiotic singing we occasionally hear of 'We'll hang out our washing on the Siegfried line, have you any dirty washing, Mother, dear.' I never heard anyone singing it.

Emily Driscoll agrees that they were grim years:

It was six years of my life and, of course, there were humorous incidents and emotional ones too, but to describe these would be a lengthy task. The thing I must stress is the spirit of people. During all our ordeals, I never once heard even a murmur that we should give in. We all felt we were quite capable of stopping Hitler and his Nazis, and Lord Haw-Haw with his 'Gairmany calling' was a joke.

Jean McWilliam takes some happy memories with her into old age . . .

. . . memories of the friendliness and togetherness of hard times, always leavened by the carefree optimism of youth and the grownups' belief that the sunlit uplands, spoken of by Churchill, would be reached in due time. Well, in a way they were, weren't they?

It is a matter of personal opinion whether the survivors of the blitz — and those many thousands who did not survive — were heroes or exploited victims. Were they proud to defend their country against the threat of Nazism, or forced into a war they wanted nothing to

208

do with? Perhaps the most important thing to remember is that — like millions of people all over the world today, in places as diverse as South Africa, Beirut and Belfast — they were thrust into the front lines of a war that was not of their making. They 'did their bit' because they had no choice.

A NOTE ON AUTHOR

Ben Wicks grew up chiefly in London's East End during the World War II, but spent two years as an evacuee in four different homes elsewhere in Britain. After leaving school at the age of fourteen, he worked in a variety of some thirty jobs, including those of a barrow boy, professional musician, commercial artist and window cleaner. He is now an international journalist, and in this capacity has travelled widely, covering the wars in Biafra and Ethiopia, the plight of refugees in the Sudan and the 1986 coup in Uganda. He is the author of eleven books, and also works as a cartoonist and a broadcaster. He lives in Toronto with his wife, Doreen; they have three children and two grandchildren. In 1986 he was awarded the Order of Canada, the country's highest civilian honour.